7 $\underline{5^{o}}$

OTHER DAYS IN GREENWICH

LIMITED EDITION

Frederick A. Hubbard

BANKSVILLE STAGE

(Photo by I. L. MEAD)

OTHER DAYS IN GREENWICH

OR

TALES AND REMINISCENCES OF
AN OLD NEW ENGLAND TOWN

BY

FREDERICK A. HUBBARD

A Heritage Classic

A Facsimile Reprint
Published 1997 by

HERITAGE BOOKS, INC.
1540E Pointer Ridge Place
Bowie, Maryland 20716
1-800-398-7709

ISBN 0-7884-0637-X

A Complete Catalog Listing Hundreds of Titles
On History, Genealogy, and Americana
Available Free Upon Request

In my days of boyhood and youth, a running mate, as we called him, belonged to every one.

There was always some congenial spirit, who shared confidences, excursions and social events, who, in school and out, was a recognized companion.

MY OLD RUNNING MATE

E. BELCHER MEAD

THIS VOLUME

IS AFFECTIONATELY DEDICATED

"I NEVER *learned the wonder of that lane,*
Drenched with the Summer rain,
Where through my boyish feet were wont to pass,
Until I left it for the passionate town,
Marble and iron and brass,
Filled with all laughter; yea, and filled, alas,
With life's immortal pain!"

CHARLES HANSON TOWNE

FREDERICK A. HUBBARD
The Author

Photo by E. Starr Sanford

CONTENTS

[xi]

CONTENTS

LIST OF ILLUSTRATIONS

LIST OF ILLUSTRATIONS

LIST OF ILLUSTRATIONS

LIST OF ILLUSTRATIONS

INTRODUCTION

This volume is not a history. It is a collection of personal reminiscences and a few stories of local interest, told to the author years ago. They all relate to the Town of Greenwich, Connecticut, where the author has resided since 1859.

He came to that town at the age of seven. All the impressive scenes of the war of '61-'65 are firmly fixed in his memory. A boy of that age is everywhere; he sees and hears everything and he never forgets.

The records of the town have always been a delight: those quaint old books that contain so many suggestions of other days. And when, years ago, the old men told stories of local events long past, they were treasured and often verified with particular dates and names.

Names and dates herein contained are believed to be correct. Certainly the dates are, as in no instance has a date been given until accuracy was first assured. The book is intensely personal. In some respects it may be deemed to be trivial. If it were a history—staid and dignified—that criticism might be just. But Daniel Merritt Mead and Spencer P. Mead are the local historians and they have done their work well.

The province of this volume is to deal with families

INTRODUCTION

and their home farms. Great farms that raised so many potatoes, years ago, that the town controlled the New York market afterwards became residence parks. Their improvement brought great wealth; new streets were laid out and from a quiet rural community Greenwich became a lively city suburb.

How this happened and when is told herein.

The photographs are included because it is believed they will be of interest. No payment for their insertion has been exacted, except the actual cost of the plate. Many dollars would have been paid for others could they have been obtained.

It has taken twenty-two years to gather the material for this book and now that the work is done the task is laid aside only with a feeling of regret.

It has been pleasant to read and talk of the other days; to imagine how some of the characters looked; of what their home life consisted; how conscientious and careful they were and to realize that in many cases, notwithstanding their restricted environment, they builded better than they knew.

Greenwich, May 1, 1913.

OTHER DAYS IN GREENWICH

CHAPTER I

THE VILLAGE

WHAT is now the Borough, with a fringe of out-
lying territory, consisted in 1859 of farms.
The Thomas A. Mead and Zaccheus Mead farms,
comprising over three hundred acres, lay to the west
and northwest of the village center. Abraham B.
Davis' farm lay to the southwest and the farms of
D. Smith Mead, Silas Merwin Mead and Dr. Theodore L. Mason were in the center, while the Philander Button, Theodore H. Mead and Titus Mead
farms lay to the northeast and east.

These farms were profitable and were managed
with all the skill which had been handed down from
generation to generation of practical farmers. Perhaps Mr. Button and Dr. Mason should be excepted
as their occupations were teaching and the practice
of medicine, farming being merely an incident. But
the others were in every sense of the word farmers
and they were good farmers, devoting their energy
and judgment to tilling their productive acres to

the best advantage. It is less than thirty years ago that Col. Mead's farm barns stood where Judge James F. Walsh's house now stands at 111 West Putnam Avenue.

Col. Thomas, as he was called for short, owned a famous herd of yellow cows and his ox barn contained several yoke of sleek oxen. The farm was known as Dearfields to which I have devoted another chapter.

The Abraham B. Davis farm adjoined Col. Mead's farm on the south. He was commonly called Benson Davis. He was a native of the town, his birthplace being at Davis Landing where the old tide mill was operated so many years and with his brother, Silas, went to New York where he made a fortune in the flour business.

In the eighteenth century the farm had belonged to William Bush. He came to Greenwich from New York about 1750. He was a young man of wealth, the only son of a retired shipping merchant. It is said that his shoe buckles were of the finest wrought silver and his small clothes were of the choicest silk. He had the swiftest horses, the finest oxen and the greatest herd of sheep and his acres were broad and fertile. The house he built was the talk of the town and upon his death, January 8, 1802, his will disposed of a large estate. He left an only daughter, Rebecca, who became the wife of John R. Cozine, from whom she obtained a divorce enabling her to convey her land as a single woman.

[2]

Daniel S. Mead

THE VILLAGE

She sold the farm to the Davises and on May 7, 1853, Abraham B. acquired from the others a complete title to the thirty acres.

I recall an antiquated colonial farmhouse that stood west of the present so-called Green Court Inn,

D. SMITH MEAD

During the last years of his life he daily drove his cows to pasture in the manner shown

which had been the homestead of William Bush before and during the war of the Revolution.

As Abraham B. Davis grew rich he desired a better house and about 1869, under the supervision of Samuel Adams, the old house was removed and the present one, known as the Green Court Inn, erected.

Here he lived summer and winter going to New York daily until his death February 4, 1879.

After the death of the widow, Eleanor R. Davis, who had acquired the farm by a will that was stubbornly contested for many months by Mr. Davis' brothers and sisters, Henry B. Marshall purchased the farm.

The farm of Daniel Smith Mead was pretty much

S. MERWIN MEAD HOMESTEAD
Built 1809

all in the village. It consisted of about one hundred and sixty acres including eleven acres now occupied by the Havemeyer School. It extended east to Davis Avenue, then called Love Lane and south to the railroad. It was a portion of a great tract of land that in the middle of the eighteenth century had belonged to Daniel Smith, the father-in-law of Daniel Smith Mead and for whom his son was named. D. Smith Mead, the grandson, lived in a house built many years ago but in 1870, when the de-

[6]

sire for the Mansard or French roof appeared its colonial form was wiped out.

The house still stands at No. 359 Greenwich Avenue and is owned by the family. The other part belonged to Silas Merwin Mead, a brother of D. Smith Mead, the second.

Merwin Mead, as he was generally called, lived in the house at No. 263 Greenwich Avenue now owned by Dr. William Burke. This house was built in 1809. The Merwin Mead farm extended north from his brother's farm along Greenwich Avenue and across to Davis Avenue. It was Merwin Mead who laid out  Elm Street and about the year 1858 planted the

S. MERWIN MEAD

elm trees that afterward suggested the name it bears. He was one of the most public spirited of the older generation. The streets that were laid out through his farm represented his contribution to the public improvement and he never asked for land damages.

The tract north of Elm Street belonged to Edwin Mead, a brother, who with Aaron Woolsey, of Bedford, N. Y., as a partner, divided the land into half acre plots then considered small and disposed of them to William Tiers, Isaac Weed and others. Mr.

[7]

Tiers lived where the Cramer building now stands and Mr. Weed lived where the library is located. What is now Rockefeller Park belonged to Henry M. Benedict, Brush Knapp and Alvan Mead.

ALVAN MEAD
1795–1883

These men owned contiguous property amounting to nearly one hundred and fifty acres, devoted to cultivation and containing two fine apple orchards.

Occasionally may be seen along Lincoln or Lexington Avenues the stump of an old tree and it is possible that in some of the back yards of the nu-

Luther Prescott Hubbard

1808-1894

merous cottages that now occupy this territory may be found a fruitful apple tree, a relic of one of the old orchards.

To me this tract is particularly interesting because in my boyhood days it constituted my trapping and hunting ground.

L. P. HUBBARD HOMESTEAD
Purchased in 1859 with savings accumulated by the non use of tobacco

My home from 1859 to 1883 was the house now owned by Dr. E. O. Parker at No. 68 East Putnam Avenue.

In the early days when the farms of which I have spoken were devoted to the business of agriculture, there were few trees to obstruct the view and from any portion of my father's home place the Sound was visible for many miles. Ancient stone walls divided

[11]

the fields that abounded in quail and meadow lark.

Piping Brook ran full before numerous drains had cut off its supply and the muskrat and an occasional mink contributed to my somewhat limited supply of pocket money.

In winter the snow often drifted over the stone walls making it possible to coast on the crust over much of this extended territory.

STEPHEN A. STOOTHOFF
1829–1911

Early in the sixties, Henry M. Benedict, in the interest of his children and incidentally in his boys' playmates, flooded a portion of his land for a skating pond.

Occasionally I walk along the streets that have cut the Benedict place in pieces and endeavor to locate some of the old haunts so familiar in other days. Recently in the backyard of one of the newly erected houses I found a remnant of the old dam and a little further south I identified the old buttonwood tree that grew near it. Mr. Benedict was devoted to his boys and his daughter, Belle, now Mrs. William C. Horn, and their wants were seldom denied.

After the skating pond was established it was thought necessary to build a small house which was warmed by a wood stove, thus enabling the children

[12]

to put on their skates in comfort. This building which was erected by Stephen A. Stoothoff, who did all Mr. Benedict's work, stood a few rods east of the

ZACCHEUS MEAD LANE 1860

rear line of Frank V. R. Reynolds' house on Mason Street.

The chapter on the Octagon house tells of Brush Knapp who owned the orchard south of the Benedict land. Lincoln Avenue now runs directly through it. There are several prominent trees on this one

[13]

hundred and fifty acre tract which still live. Near what is now called Putnam Terrace stood an ash tree whose trunk was twelve feet in circumference. It was considered a detriment to the Sound view many years ago and was cut down, but near the home of Miss Amelia Knapp may be seen small trees of this variety which have sprung from the roots of the parent tree. Two or three buttonball trees graced the landscape but they are all gone except the remains of the one near the old dam.

The great oak tree now on the front lawn of B. Frank Finney, on Mason Street, was a popular shelter for the cows that were pastured in that field and the triplet-trunk silver maple on the corner of Mason Street and Lexington Avenue looks just as it did fifty years ago.

When the autumn days came all the boys were interested in nut gathering. The Mason farm had several fine hickory trees, one of which still stands on the front lawn of Frank V. R. Reynolds' place. Another stands in the rear of Dr. J. A. Clark's place on Mason Street and the remains of one that was on the Merwin Mead farm still stands on the corner of Mason and Elm Streets.

Dr. Mason was engaged in the active practice of his profession in Brooklyn and his farm was managed by George Wellner, whose name I learned years afterwards; a good hearted German who must have emigrated to this country late in life as he spoke very broken English. We called him Dutch

[14]

George, having heard others call him by that name, and he never resented it.

He was inclined to tease us sometimes but always acceded to our request for the privilege of gather-

DEEP HOLE 1860

ing nuts on the Mason farm. Longer excursions for nuts took us down Zaccheus Mead's lane and to the chestnut trees near "Sheep Pen" on the Thomas A. Mead farm.

It will therefore appear that the one hundred and fifty acre parcel I have described did not include all the playground of the boys of those times. It was our immediate reservation but frequently we made excursions to the east across what is now Milbank to

[15]

Theodore H. Mead's brook (called the brook "Brothers"), for a swim.

Then the notion would take us in the other direction across Col. Mead's farm to "Sheep Pen," a famous swimming hole long ago filled up with sand because there were no more sheep to wash. Sometimes we enjoyed a picnic, perched on the rocky sides of Deep Hole, a rustic spot that is practically unchanged. Occasionally we walked down Love Lane, now Davis Avenue, to the old tide mill and under its protecting shadow undressed and dove from the rocks still visible north of the causeway.

In those days there was no road across the dam. What is now Bruce Park was the Isaac Howe Mead farm and behind a great ledge of rocks, on the westerly side of the pond, long since removed, we felt that bathing clothes were quite superfluous. The Davis pond was always popular as a bathing place because no account need be taken of the tide. At low water the gate was down and the pond was full.

CHAPTER II

THE preceding chapter has dealt with some of the rural parts of Greenwich, but no allusion has been made to its commercial interests.

These interests were so insignificant that they are mentioned only to make the story of Greenwich complete. Before and during the war of 1861, it is my impression that Newman & Hewes of Mianus, in their general store did more business than all others combined.

The Upper Landing, as Mianus is still called, was a busy place and from thence most of our farm products were shipped. Joseph Brush, at Cos Cob also did a large business.

The village of Greenwich was not without stores and although they were called general stores they were not conducted like the general store in prosperous communities at the present time. Remote places in New England have such stores to-day as we had fifty years ago.

Putnam Avenue was then called Main Street, the successor of the main country road, a name that had been used for many generations. At the corner of

[17]

Putnam Avenue and Sherwood Place, then called
Mechanic Street, was the business center for a number
of years.   Under President James Buchanan the post
office had been located in what is now known as Dr.
Frank M. Holly's cottage and Squire Samuel Close
was postmaster.   But when President Lincoln was

POST OFFICE 1859

elected the office of postmaster went to Joseph E.
Brush and the office, about six feet square, was
opened in the building now owned and occupied by
Frederick Denson.

Mr. Brush and later Brush & Wright, Benjamin
Wright being the partner, ran a general store.
They kept everything but fresh meats, including dry

[18]

goods, paints, oils, a general line of groceries and a limited stock of hardware and crockery.

On the opposite corner stood the old Congregational Church a large frame structure which had been moved in 1860 after the construction of the present

POST OFFICE 1861

stone edifice. Col. Thomas A. Mead and his nephew, Amos M. Brush, were the owners of the property. It stood on the northeast corner of Putnam Avenue and Sherwood Place and was occupied by Dr. James Aiken's drug store, Linus Weed's jewelry store, the law office of Julius B. Curtis and the town offices. The upper floor was a public hall, where were held

[19]

many spirited meetings and lectures during the time of the war.

In what is now the front door yard of Dr. Virgil C. Piatti's residence, close to the street line, stood a small one-story building, used as a meat market by John Henderson. It stood on land leased of Dr. Mason and was not removed till about 1870.

Abram Acker kept a grocery store in a two-story frame building that stood where the eastern end of the Lenox House now stands. The old building was removed to the rear of the present structure in 1873 and was converted into servants' quarters for the hotel. It still stands there.

JOSEPH E. BRUSH
1817–1886
Wartime Postmaster

Peter Acker, a brother of Abram Acker, for many years conducted a grocery store in a frame building, standing where Isaac L. Mead's building is now located, on the corner of Putnam and Greenwich Avenues. A piazza ran across the south side of this building from which was a fine view of Long Island Sound. It was reached by a long flight of steps which afforded a comfortable roosting place for a lot of genial fellows, who would occasionally crawl down the stairs and through a cellar door that was always

invitingly open. Expensive bars were then unknown hereabouts, and a draught of New England

John Dayton

rum did not come amiss, although served across the
head of a barrel.

Matthew Mead kept a cobbler's shop nearly opposite the John A. Bullard garage.

Benjamin Peck, and later Frank Holmes, con-

ducted a dry-goods store in a large frame building
which for many years after was occupied by the
Greenwich Savings Bank, standing on what is now
Mrs. L. P. Jones' land.

FIRST BUSINESS BUILDING ERECTED ON GREENWICH
AVENUE 1854

John Dayton, who died August 18, 1908, was the
first man to venture the purchase of a lot on Greenwich Avenue for business purposes. He was thought
to be injudicious when he and Daniel Merritt Mead,
as a partner, paid $500 for a lot 50x150. On this
land they built the frame building now occupied by
the Greenwich Savings Bank. The first floor was
the Dayton shoe store and Counselor Mead con-

ducted a law office in the second story which was subsequently used for many years by Col. Heusted W. R. Hoyt for the same purpose.

Peter Acker's garden lay along the west side of the avenue down to the grocery store of Oliver Lockwood, whose stand was where Benjamin Lockwood's restaurant and Arthur Phillips' store are now located.

Henry Held conducted the only meat market on Greenwich Avenue and that was open only during the forenoon. It occupied the frame building now owned by S. A. and H. L. Brush at No. 74. It was not profitable to keep the store open in the afternoon and evening, the business being insufficient. No deliveries were made and many of the people of wealth, for those days, carried their purchases home.

John H. Merritt's fish market, which also served home-made ice cream in the hot weather, stood on Capt. Wm. L. Lyon's land, where the Trust Co.'s building now stands. Later it was moved across the street and is now occupied as a plumber's store by Elias S. Peck.

These stores were all the village had. Even the tinner and the plumber were missing. There was little for a plumber to do, there being no public water supply. If a tea kettle needed repair or a house required tinning, Port Chester artisans did the work, unless a traveling tinker happened to call.

It was not till nearly the close of the war that William and Robert Talbot, brothers, arrived and opened a plumbing and tinning shop at the head of the avenue on land then belonging to Jacob T. Weed and still in the possession of his family. The building was removed several years ago. A number of descendants of the Talbot brothers are well-known residents of the Borough.

With no street lights, very few side walks, and they of the crudest kind, it is easy to realize what a quiet country village Greenwich was during the war. Very few ventured out at night and those who went to an evening meeting or to pay a social call usually carried a lantern. Moonlight nights were always counted on and when the snow was on the ground coasting and sleigh-riding were greatly enjoyed.

CHAPTER III

THE previous chapters have dealt with the village and its immediate surroundings, but no allusion has been made to the township.

There are many who have no idea of the territorial extent of Greenwich. It is nearly as large as the District of Columbia. Before the days of rural free mail delivery it had a half dozen post offices and to-day it has four railway stations—Greenwich, Cos Cob, Riverside and Sound Beach.

In 1859 it was a farming community producing hay, grain, potatoes, apples and milk in such quantities that its population had become wealthy. The farms were generally unincumbered and railroad, bank and insurance stocks were largely held. Of course in those days the measure of wealth was much smaller than at present but most of the farmers were worth fifty thousand dollars, besides their farms valued at about one hundred dollars an acre.

The population was about 6,500 and the assessed valuation for taxation was $2,882,353 which included nine hundred and ninety-seven houses valued at $701,580, showing that about three-fourths of the taxes were levied on farm lands, and that therein lay the importance of the town.

OTHER DAYS IN GREENWICH

As I have shown, Mianus had more commercial interests than Horse Neck, the usual name for the village.

ABRAHAM REYNOLDS
1830–1908

The "Lower Landing," or Cos Cob, had its market boats, as well as Mianus and from these two points most of the farm products found their way to the city. Capt. Daniel Merritt at Piping Point, near the foot of Arch Street (the landing having been covered by the present railroad embankment), and Capt. Caleb Holmes at Rocky Neck had all they could do in the transportation of produce, but the other side of the town outnumbered them in freight tonnage.

Oliver Mead, Thomas A. Mead, Stephen L. Radford, Zaccheus Mead, Charles Mead, Abraham and Augustus N. Reynolds of North Street and their neighbors, Lot and Drake Mead, were a few of the large shippers of farm produce.

CAPT. CALEB HOLMES
1812–1887

Milk went away by train every night in large quantities, while now not a can goes out but instead many cans are imported from the northern counties of New York and Massachusetts.

Ignoring, for the present the territory north of the Parsonage Road, it may be interesting to recall the various farms that composed that part of the town now included in its thickly settled southern portion, exclusive of the village.

At Byram, and on the point of the same name, including very much of East Port Chester were the farms of Jonas Mead and Daniel Lyon. That part of the town was in closer communication with Port Chester than with our own village but on the Sabbath day Deacon Jonas Mead, his sons, Mark and Milo, and three old ladies with poke bonnets, seemingly representatives of generations long departed were regular attendants at the Second Congregational Church.

AUGUSTUS N. REYNOLDS

The Lyons were, I think, Episcopalians and attended church in Port Chester.

Sunday consisted of sacred and solemn hours and its observance was strict.

Now that houses, some very large and expensive and many of more modest proportions cover this territory it is hard to realize how beautifully rural

Byram Point was half a century ago. Thrusting its head above a rugged ledge in which its roots are fastened an ancient cedar tree may be occasionally seen, a relic of the wild and artistic growth that finally at-

STEPHEN L. RADFORD
1828-1907

tracted such purchasers as William J. Tingue and Charles and Henry R. Mallory. The soil between the out cropping rocks was extremely fertile and those patient, plodding farmers wrested what they considered a fortune from the land which later produced to

[28]

their descendants sudden and marvelous wealth in the quick turning of real estate deals.

Milo Mead has been called the Sage of New Lebanon, his name for East Port Chester. His father, Deacon Jonas Mead, died August 2, 1871.

His estate consisted of about seven thousand dol-

JONAS MEAD HOMESTEAD
Torn down 1911

lars in personal property and one hundred and forty-two and one-half acres of land appraised at $40,000. This land went to his two sons, Mark and Milo, but remained undivided until January, 1879, when all the shore front consisting of thirty acres and much land besides was set off to Mark Mead while his brother,

Milo, had to content himself with inland property, although eight acres had a frontage on the Byram River, where the New Lebanon docks were afterwards built.

Upon acquiring this land, Milo Mead had it sur-

MILO MEAD 1904

veyed and divided into lots fifty feet wide, naming the whole Meadville. Subsequently this name was abandoned and the name New Lebanon adopted and persistently adhered to down to the day of his death, August 2, 1906. Once when asked the significance of the name, he stated that the cedars reminded him of those in Lebanon of Bible history.

However, the name was never popular. The merchants preferred East Port Chester and William J.

Tingue favored Hawthorne, after his woolen mills at Glenville. For a short time the post office bore this latter name. The school district was called New Lebanon in consideration of a gift of valuable land for school purposes.

Henry A. Merritt could purchase the river front only upon condition that the dock he contemplated building should be called the New Lebanon dock, which name it still retains. The Opera House, the Danish club house and the town dock, located on land given by Mr. Mead, and a few places of business, still bear the name.

DEACON JONAS MEAD

The Danish club house is Mr. Mead's best monument. He gave the land and furnished the money for its construction. In front of the building, which is of brick, with stone trimmings, is a bronze bas relief of Mr. Mead and beneath it the inscription "The Sage of New Lebanon."

It is a work of art and a very correct likeness, though so high in the wall that it is seldom noticed. The artist was Carla Christensen, a young lady of Copenhagen.

There is a large population of Danes in East Port

Chester, and they held Mr. Mead in high esteem, primarily because he was willing to dispose of his land to them at reasonable prices when he might have sold to much better advantage to the wealthy for large estates.

The thirty-acre tract of Sound Shore front set off to Mark Mead was quickly sold and is now occupied by such places as those of Joseph Milbank, John H. Hanan, Charles Mallory and Edgar L. Marston, president of the Farmers' Loan and Trust Co.

WINDSOR CHAIR

Used by Deacon Jonas Mead and his son Milo. Now the property of the Author

Farther west was the farm of John R. Grigg, somewhat remote because what is now Hamilton Avenue with a trolley line was but a right of way with gates now and then. But his broad fields were none the less productive and all his life he devoted himself to their cultivation. The old white farmhouse, still standing, was then a landmark all by itself, commanding a broad view of Long Island Sound. But it has been dwarfed and rendered insignificant by great three-story Italian apartment houses and by numerous mod-

[32]

ern cottages in the near-by Jaynes Park, a portion of the original farm.

Just across the valley, on the next ridge to the east, was the farm of Augustus Mead. The old homestead moved back a few rods from the street and enlarged is now known as Homestead Hall, a popular summer hotel. Open the town records of fifty years ago and almost every page reveals his name. He was a careful, methodical, and thrifty farmer of ample means and possessing the characteristics of wisdom and moderation. He was a man of deliberate judgment and those who had no claims upon him, ex-

JOHN P. GRIGG

cept that they were his townsmen went to him for advice and counsel.

I do not intend to imply that he was not progressive; only that always before he made a move he was sure of his ground. Those who were his contemporaries say that he was a close reader of scientific publications and that he gave careful attention to the products of the patent office. Any new devices in farming implements particularly interested him and in his outbuildings were many examples of oddly constructed plows and harrows with which he had experimented. He was a thorough believer in any change of methods suggestive of progress. He was the first man to build an ice house in town.

He held various offices of trust including the initial judgeship of the Court of Probate. I recall exactly

JUDGE AUGUSTUS MEAD
About 1860

how he looked as he drove along in a square box wagon and tied his brown horse, Dandy, to a stone post standing under a great elm tree, whose branches still hang over the little building that held the Probate Court and the Post Office. His name has been perpetuated in his son, Augustus I. Mead, and his grandson, Augustus, son of Nelson B. Mead.

I can not refrain at this point from digressing a little to tell the story of the Post Office building, as revealed in the town records, showing as it does the confidence in business matters enjoyed by the men of those days. Samuel Close was postmaster in 1859.

HOMESTEAD OF AUGUSTUS MEAD AS IT APPEARED IN 1859

He had succeeded Isaac Weed in 1831 and, with the exception of four years prior to 1854, when Joseph E. Brush was postmaster, held the office till the election of President Lincoln in 1860. He and Judge Mead were the leaders in their party and it fell to them to arrange for quarters for the new Judge of Probate. Mr. Close then owned the property at 20 East Putnam Avenue now owned by Dr. Frank M. Holly.

As soon as Augustus Mead was elected Judge of Probate he hired of Mr. Close the northeast corner of his door yard and, at his own expense, erected a frame building which is still standing. The lease was executed December 3, 1853. It recites the fact that Judge Mead had already erected the building. The lease provided that it should be used only for the office of town clerk, the post office and Court of Probate. As the building was only 20x28 the limitation of its use seems to have been hardly necessary.

SQUIRE SAM'L CLOSE
In 1860

The postmaster was to have the exclusive right to occupy the first story, but not to interfere with Judge Mead in passing through in order to get to the second story, which indicates the location of the Probate Court and carries with it the suggestion that Mr. Close received his ground rent in the partial use of the building erected by Judge Mead.

Judge Mead died April 22, 1864, still the nominal owner of the building. In the settlement of his estate, although the building was a fixture and actually belonged to Mr. Close as the lease had terminated October 1, 1858, it was appraised in the estate of Judge Mead at $300. On June 8, 1864, Elkanah Mead, as administrator of Judge Mead's estate, sold the building, at the appraisal, to Rebecca R. Mayo, the wife of Captain Thomas Mayo and the daughter of Mr. Close. Dr. Holly has improved and greatly enlarged the building making it a very tasty cottage.

The front wing represents the original building and the identical letter slot is still at the left of the front door.

But the great farm, the farm with a history, was owned by Oliver Mead and a portion of it is now known as Field Point Park. To-day it is beautiful with its fine residences, its sweeping lawns and its brilliant flower beds, visible from the water, the growth of trees and foliage having cut off the view from any other point. But all its rural simplicity has departed. It lies like an over-turned spoon one hundred and ten acres south of the homestead, and once from any part of it the view of Sound and village was unobstructed. Those who live on the charming outer circle of this wonderful point have all the view they desire.

There are ancient oak trees on this land, some of them perhaps of the forest primeval. There were springs, some very close to the shore, where the cattle drank and where the Round Hill and Stanwich picknickers filled their pails. The stone walls were in many places ten feet wide, blasted from the land by the first settler, Zophar Mead.

Years before the Revolution all the territory between Horse Neck Brook and the extremity of the Point was common land—a great horse pasture, into which any of the inhabitants could turn their horses. The early records call it "Horse Neck Field Point"

[37]

from which the original name of the village, Horse Neck, was derived.

In the latter part of the eighteenth century Abraham Mead conducted a pottery where the Held House now stands. He had two sons, Isaac and Zophar. The latter settled on the lower portion of Field Point and was the father of Oliver. Isaac settled on the northern portion and was the father of Augustus Mead. It was the understanding between the sons that their father should divide his time between them. When the old place at Indian Harbor was given up Abraham Mead went to live with his son Isaac, dying before the first year of his residence with him had expired.

Abraham Mead was a devout and influential member of the Second Congregational Church and to distinguish him from some of the other Meads with the same given name, he was called Deacon Potter from his occupation.

But to return to the southerly portion of Field Point where Oliver Mead was born and died. When I was a boy he was a man of inferior physical strength, living in the old homestead, a bachelor, but surrounded with all the comforts that his life required. He moved about the farm slowly and painfully, leaning upon a cane and giving to his men intelligent directions for their work. He was noted for his fine oxen of which he had several yoke, as a pair was called. He frequently loaned to his neighbors his oxen, but it was said that he was so solicitous

OLIVER MEAD HOMESTEAD

In 1859

for their welfare that he sent a double team or two pair when but one pair was requested. Every portion of Field Point was under the most careful cultivation.

The old oak trees still standing along the easterly shore, now owned by George F. Dominick and perhaps some others, and one or two on the extreme point now owned by Seymour J. Hyde, were his pride. On one occasion he spoke of them as shading his cultivated land to its damage, but added that he could well afford the diminished crops, the trees were so grand.

Mr. Mead never took any active part in public affairs. He was a member of the Second Congregational Church and a liberal giver to every worthy benevolent cause. He died March 19, 1887, at the age of 87 years.

MISS SALLY MEAD
For many years in the family of Oliver Mead

In addition to Field Point he owned Round Island and considerable other land. The inventory of his estate shows 166 acres of land valued at $64,300 and $108,076.22 of personalty.

For years the eyes of wealthy men had been on

Field Point, with its fine shore front, more than a mile in extent. Occasionally it was reported that Mr. Mead had been offered large sums to part with this land, some of which he had bought, but most of

OLIVER MEAD

which was ancestral estate. But the old man, feeble as he was, outlived many who had coveted those broad acres.

When he died his last will, dated December 1, 1882, was filed for probate and at once a most interesting discussion arose among both lawyers and

[42]

laymen as to what disposition he had made of the land.

His cousin, Oliver D. Mead, now president of the Greenwich National Bank, had lived with Oliver Mead for several years before his death and the old man had enjoyed, during that time, the comfort and solace of the younger man's wife and daughters. But some of the lawyers said that Oliver D. Mead had only a life estate in this fine property and was not able to convey a perfect fee title. Others took

POTTERY MADE BY DEACON ABRAHAM MEAD 1790

the opposite view and while the discussion was rife no one cared to purchase, whatever his own opinion of the matter might be. The cause of contention was the seventeenth clause of the will which I venture to quote in full.

"I give, devise and bequeath all my real estate, "wheresoever situated including my burial plot, all my "stock and farming utensils on said real estate, all "my household furniture of every description and all "my wearing apparel to Oliver D. Mead to him and "to his heirs forever. If the said Oliver D. Mead

"should die without leaving any heirs, then and in
"that event I give my said real estate to Augustus
"I. Mead to him and his heirs forever."

While the discussion continued Oliver D. Mead
was in possession, certainly with perfect propriety,
for at least he had a life estate. But it was no easy
burden in the days of unprofitable farming to
carry on such a farm and pay the taxes; at least that
is my own conclusion.

Under these circumstances it was quite natural for
Mr. Mead to welcome a possible purchaser for at
least a portion of the property whatever the title.
Therefore, in the spring of 1895, a proposition was
made that the town purchase Round Island including a considerable parcel on the main land for a public park. The price fixed was seventy-five thousand
dollars. A special meeting was held on the eighth of
April and resulted in the appointment of a committee
of purchase, consisting of George G. McNall, John
H. Banks and Sheldon E. Minor.

The deed was signed but was never delivered, because many of the residents of Belle Haven believed
that the extension of the shore road to the island which
was contemplated in the deal and the maintenance of
a public park at that place would be undesirable.
Influence from many sources was brought to bear on
the parties interested and it was concluded to aban-
don the matter. It has been a great regret to many
who at the time opposed it, that the park was not
established and especially since it has become known

that John D. Chapman, the present owner of Round Island paid very much more and bought considerably less land than was contemplated in the park scheme.

But there came a time, three years later, when the question of title went to the courts and our Supreme Court of Errors decided that Oliver D. Mead's title was perfect.

The case arose upon a contract for the sale of a portion of the land which had first been purchased by Judge R. Jay Walsh who contracted to sell it to James McCutcheon. The latter took the ground that Judge Walsh had an imperfect title and could not carry out his contract to convey the fee of the land. Probably as far as these litigants were concerned, the suit was a friendly one, the sole object being to have the will reviewed and its meaning determined by the highest Court in Connecticut. But when the matter actually got into court other interests were cited in; the arguments of all the counsel were very full and complete and appearances indicated that the suit could scarcely be termed friendly but one in which those interested wanted all that belonged to them.

The case first went to the Superior Court and without the introduction of testimony the following finding of facts was agreed upon.

"That Oliver D. Mead derived his title to Field "Point under the will of his cousin, Oliver Mead. "That at the time of the execution of the will Oliver "D. Mead and his three children were living and are "still living. That Augustus I. Mead is living and "that he has two children. That Oliver Mead de-"rived his title from his father, Zophar Mead, by will "in 1844 and that Zophar Mead derived title to a "portion of the farm from his father Abraham Mead, "in 1827. Upon the death of Oliver Mead, Oliver "D. and his family were in possession of the farm, "having been living there some time in the control "and management of the property. Both the father "and mother of Augustus I. Mead were first cousins "of Oliver Mead. Oliver Mead's nearest relations "were first cousins. He was never married."

Under the 17th section of the will, previously quoted, Samuel Fessenden of Stamford, arguing for the defendant, claimed that Oliver D. Mead took an absolute title and that the provision regarding the death of Oliver D. "without leaving any heirs" was intended only to provide for the contingency of Oliver D. dying before the death of Oliver. That the intent must govern unless it is contrary to law. He claimed that the 17th section of the will in connection with the 19th section and surrounding circumstances clearly indicated that it was the intention of the testator to create an absolute estate.

The 19th section of the will reads as follows: "If "there should not be enough estate outside of what I "have given to Oliver D. Mead to pay all the legacies "($86,000) then and in that event I order and direct "the executor hereinafter appointed to pay each pro "rata. If any of the legatees should die before my

[46]

"decease, then and in that event, the legacy I have
"given to such legatee or legatees, I give and devise
"to the heirs of such deceased legatee or legatees."

Taking the two sections Mr. Fessenden argued that
it was the intention of Oliver Mead to leave the real
estate to Oliver D., provided he outlived him. If he
died before the testator, leaving heirs, he intended
that they should inherit the estate absolutely. If
Oliver D. died before Oliver, leaving no heirs, then
it was intended that Augustus I. Mead should take
the land absolutely. A legatee is one who takes personal property under a will and a devisee is one who
takes land. The counsel argued that these two
words had been employed by the testator without
distinguishing any difference in their meaning.
Hence, he claimed that the 19th section included the
devise to Oliver D. Mead, when he provided that the
children of such legatees should take, if the legatee
died before the death of the testator, showing that
the second half of the 17th section of the will was
only to provide against a lapse of the devise. He
reasoned that the provision in the 19th section that
"If there should not be enough outside of what he
had given Oliver D. to pay all the legacies they were
to be paid pro rata" showed conclusively that Oliver
intended Oliver D. to take the farm unincumbered
and untrammeled by any burden whatsoever.

In reply, John E. Keeler, of Stamford, argued
that Oliver D. Mead did not acquire an absolute title
to the land devised to him under the will. He said:

"To support the view that Oliver D. Mead became possessed of an absolute title, it is necessary to claim one of two things, either that all of the 17th section after the first sentence is to be rejected as repugnant and of no meaning; or that the words 'die without leaving any heirs' refer to Oliver D. Mead's death before the death of the testator, Oliver Mead.

"It cannot be seriously contended that all of the "second sentence is to be set aside as having no mean-"ing. Evidently the testator had two methods of "disposition in mind as relating to his real estate, "turning upon the time of the death of Oliver D. "Mead.

"If the latter died before him he desired the "property to go immediately to his heirs in fee; these "heirs were children of Oliver D. Mead in being at "the time of the making of the will; but if Oliver D. "Mead died after Oliver Mead leaving no children "then an entirely different disposition takes place and "Augustus I. Mead succeeds to the property."

Mr. John C. Chamberlain, of Bridgeport, representing Augustus I. Mead and his children, argued that Oliver D. Mead had an estate tail in the land, relying largely upon a case decided by the same Court in June, 1896, entitled Chestro vs. Palmer, 58 Conn. Reports, page 207, in which the construction of a will was sought, the will reading quite like the will of Oliver Mead. "In that case the Court de-"cided that the estate created by the will was only an

"estate tail and that the whole situation was so sim-
"ilar to that found in Chestro vs. Palmer that it is
"apparently impossible to construe this estate in
"Oliver D. Mead to be anything more than a fee tail,
"without overruling all the law of the State upon the
"subject."

Mr. Chamberlain's contention concerning the
rights of Augustus I. Mead in the property was
much wider than the claim made by Mr. Keeler.
While Mr. Keeler recognized the possible accession
to the land by the children and grandchildren of
Oliver D. Mead, Mr. Chamberlain argued that the
"remainder," after the death of Oliver D. Mead,
would go to Augustus I. Mead and that the descendants of Oliver D. Mead would have no interest after
the death of their father. Answering Mr. Fessenden with relation to a provision of the testator in the
19th section whereby the legacies were to be paid
pro rata if there should not be money enough, Mr.
Chamberlain said that the clause was not inconsistent
with his claim. "Oliver Mead had entailed the land
"and it was to go to future generations, hence it
"could not be sold to pay legacies but must be kept
"intact."

Nor did he think that possession and occupation
of the premises by Oliver D. Mead before the death
of Oliver Mead was inconsistent with the theory that
Oliver Mead intended his cousin to occupy the place
for life.

"The property was partly ancestral estate and if
"there had been no will Augustus I. Mead and his
"brother, Nelson B. Mead, would have taken the land
"to the exclusion of Oliver D. Mead, and it is not
"strange that the old man desired it to remain in the
"same branch of the family from whence it had come
"to him."

Chief Justice Andrews wrote the opinion in which
he pursued much the same method of reasoning as
did Mr. Fessenden in his argument. I quote from
the opinion.

"The language in the 17th paragraph, in its first
"clause, creates in Oliver D. Mead an absolute es-
"tate in fee simple, in the lands in question. This
"Court in a very recent case, Mansfield vs. Shelton,
"67 Conn. Reports, page 390, and after an exam-
"ination of the prior cases, held that an express gift
"in fee simple will not be reduced to a life estate by
"mere implication from a subsequent gift over, but
"may be by subsequent language clearly indicating
"intent and equivalent to a positive provision.

"The words of the second clause of the 17th para-
"graph, which are supposed to have the effect of re-
"ducing the fee simple title created in Oliver D.
"Mead to a lesser estate are: 'If the said Oliver D.
"Mead should die without leaving any heir, then,
"&c.' Read literally these words mean nothing.
"No man can die without leaving any heirs. The
"law presumes, until the contrary is shown, that
"every deceased person leaves heirs. It is argued

[50]

"that the word heirs ought to be read as meaning chil-
"dren.

.   .   .   .

"In a suitable case the Court might possibly adopt
"such a reading. But in the present case, where the
"effect of the changed reading would be to defeat
"the very clearly expressed general intent of the tes-
"tator, as well as to reduce an express gift in fee
"simple to a lesser estate, the Court would hardly
"feel authorized to do so. . . . There is another
"rule of construction which has been followed many
"times by this Court, and which is decisive of this
"case. It is, that when in a will an estate in fee is
"followed by an apparently inconsistent limitation,
"the whole should be reconciled by reading the latter
"disposition as applying exclusively to the event of
"the prior devisee in fee dying in the lifetime of the
"testator. The intention of the testator being, it is
"considered, to provide a substituted devisee in a case
"of a lapse. This construction gives effect to all the
"words of the will and makes all its parts consistent.
"The reference in the 19th clause to the estate 'given
"to Oliver D. Mead' was evidently intended to cover
"whatever was disposed of by the 17th clause. Part
"of that—the personal estate—was unquestionably
"an absolute gift. It is therefore reasonable to sup-
"pose that as the testator in this reference made no
"discrimination, he had intended none, between the
"real and personal property, and understood that he
"had given an absolute estate in both.

[51]

"It is also to be considered that if the provision "for Oliver's death without leaving any heirs were "read as one as to his death without leaving any sur- "viving issue, whether it occurred either before or "after that of the testator, then it contemplated a "devise to such issue, which would be void under the "former statute of perpetuities.

"The construction which we adopt, on the other "hand, by confining the effect of this clause to a "death before that of the testator, makes this clause "valid and satisfies the rule that when a devise may "fairly be read either as a legal or an illegal one, the "former meaning is preferred.

"From all the words of the will examined in the "light of the circumstances, we are persuaded that "Oliver Mead intended by his will to give, and did "give, to Oliver D. Mead an estate in fee simple in "all his lands."

This decision was generally satisfactory among those disinterested. It was suggested by some that the opinion was strained in the interest of an expedi- ency. It is true that the public interests would not be conserved by tying up for many years such a valuable tract of land and a feeling of satisfaction was manifest, when it became known that Field Point had been purchased by a corporation known as the Field Point Land Co., for the purpose of develop- ment. The deed executed by Oliver D. Mead recited a nominal consideration but the actual consideration

was probably greater than in any other of our recorded conveyances.

Sales of the land were consummated as soon as
the company had laid out the property, and introduced light, water, sewerage and roads. It has been
said that the land sold, all of which had shore front,
brought from ten to fifteen thousand dollars an acre
and no lot was sold less than three acres in area.

CHAPTER IV

BEFORE taking up another farm that made rural Greenwich in other days, the old white bridge occurs to me as a subject for this chapter. It may serve to break the monotony of my story.

Davis' Creek is spanned by a railroad bridge near the new pumping station, like scores of others along the line. But in 1859, a covered bridge of heavy frame, shingle roofed and shaped like a spireless church covered the creek above the old mill. It was then about eleven years old. It was painted a glistening white and with the exception of the black smirches at the top from the belching smoke stacks was kept as neat and clean as a country church.

Engineers on the night trains have often told how, as soon as they rounded the curve leaving Cos Cob, the white bridge would loom up before them, apparently double its actual size and glistening like a snow bank in the moonlight. None of the trainmen ever had any affection for the white bridge. It stood in a spot, until within thirty years, the most isolated between New York and Springfield. Overhanging hills covered with scrub oaks and tall cedars, but revealing white, spectral-like tombstones in the old

[54]

THE WHITE BRIDGE—1861

THE WHITE BRIDGE

Davis burying ground, were on the north, while on the other sides the diversity of forest and meadow land, which in the glow of daylight were romantic in the extreme, at night were weird and uncanny enough.

The white bridge was removed about 1880, but like its neighbor, the old mill, it had been a landmark for many a day.

Queer stories were often told by superstitious engineers of the goblins that played at night about the old bridge and swung their spectral lanterns before the cab windows as the locomotive leaped into the resounding and trembling structure.

In the daytime the place was often frequented by school children—by those who ought to have been at school. Girls and boys alike would scurry across the ties as a train rounded the curve and hiding behind the great timbers of the bridge would hold on to the iron braces till the train had thundered through. It was a dangerous spot and eleven lives were the toll of the white bridge.

Besides the ghost stories that the trainmen used to tell about the bridge, there was one tale told of this spot that was really true.

About the year 1860 the night train for Boston, consisting of baggage express and sleeping cars, was made up at 27th Street and hauled by horses through the Park Avenue tunnel to 42nd Street. Here, while the cars were being coupled in what was a far uptown street, surrounded by the whitewashed cabins of squatters, the home of goats and thieves, the express car was boarded by two robbers. How they were able to force the door and get into the car no one can tell, but they succeeded either by the aid of a confederate trainman or by mere chance. Some have said that the door was carelessly left open and that the thieves, happening to be about, saw their opportunity and seized it. Be that as it may they got into the car and shut the door after them.

The car was filled with treasure—government bonds, bank notes and bags upon bags of gold coin. No one was ever able or willing to tell just how many millions of dollars was in that rolling treasure house that night.

As the train started on its trip how the thieves must have exulted in their rich find! The boxes and bags in which the securities and gold were packed, were immediately broken open and their contents examined with care. Many bags of gold and packages of bank notes were piled up by the door and the non-negotiable bonds and other securities were left in a litter upon the floor. The gold and bank notes could be safely handled and of these there was a fortune larger than the wildest fancy of the thieves had ever conceived of. What use then to bother with securities that probably were registered? These, representing millions of dollars which the robbers trampled in the reeling car were to them of no more value than so much brown paper. They were surfeited with the wealth of gold and bank notes.

The first stop to be made was at the Cos Cob drawbridge, where all trains paused, and this the thieves probably knew, indeed they seem to have been familiar with the country about the white bridge, as the circumstances I am about to narrate will show.

As the train approached this secluded spot the robbers began to unload the car. The bags of gold and bundles of bank notes were thrown out as though an immense scoop had shoveled them through the door. For a mile the track was littered with wealth. As the train moved across the Cos Cob bridge, the robbers had alighted, leaving the door open. This was observed at Stamford and the robbery reported.

Every effort was made to recover the treasure and to apprehend the robbers but not a clew was left to their identity. They were never apprehended.

Some of the money came to light and in the most peculiar places. Bundles of bank notes were found in hollow trees and bags of gold to a large amount were found secreted among the upper truss beams of the white bridge. It was here indeed that the largest amount of the stolen treasure was discovered, for the robbers had evidently believed it a safe bank in which temporarily to deposit their ill-gotten hoard. And it doubtless would have been had not the jarring of a train shaken one of the canvas bags filled with gold almost into the lap of a young lady who had baited her line for crabs beneath the old bridge.

For many years the railroad men called the present

bridge, without roof and painted black, the "white bridge" after the one that really was white.

About the old white bridge more tales cluster than I could tell in a day. Tales of ball games in the Lyman Mead meadow near by, now fenced in as a part of Milbank; tales of love and tales of greed.

Many of my readers will remember that summer night in 1876 when the old bridge was filled with boulders and cross ties into which the shore line express ran with terrible force. That no blood was shed that night was the will of a kind Providence, which protected the unconscious occupants of the long line of sleeping cars that waited while the trainmen tumbled the obstructions into the creek below. And the same protection perhaps enabled the villains who had planned a robbery to escape to the woods, where the engineer saw them stumbling across the graves in the Davis Cemetery.

But no recollections of the white bridge are pleasanter than to those who remember it as a rendezvous for crabbers.

In the quiet days of September when the haze of autumn rested on the creek and veiled the woods beyond, who has not, in other days, stretched himself upon the bit of sand beneath the railway bank, now covered by the pump house, and waited for the lazy bite of the succulent crab? But the crabs are as scarce these days as the gold in the span of the new white bridge.

CHAPTER V

BANKSVILLE AND STANWICH

BANKSVILLE lies at the extreme northern edge of the town. It has a church of quaint construction. The post office is in a village store, located a few feet over the line, in the State of New York.

The outlook of the village is towards the north where the wooded hills of North Castle and Middle Patent are in full sight. The water courses all run to the north and eventually join the waters of the Mianus.

Many years ago—perhaps seventy—when shoe-making was all done by hand, the village of Banks-ville was largely engaged in that industry. For thirty years or more it kept in touch with Greenwich through the Banksville stage, which carried mail and passengers. Silas Derby, the owner of the line, was a quaint old character who passed away some years ago but who was well-known by the older generation. His mode of dress, the trim of his whiskers and his cheery "Yap" to his steeds will be readily recalled.

Several years ago a busy South Street merchant enquired whether Derby was still driving the Banks-ville stage and being answered in the affirmative he went on to say:

"When I was a young lad my grandmother, who

lived on the west road, Stanwich, would send me out to meet the stage for the mail as it made its daily trip. Often through the summer, I made the trip to the steamboat dock, fished all day and came back with Derby at night. Recently I had occasion to again visit Greenwich, after an absence of twenty years,

CHURCH AT BANKSVILLE

and there was dear old Derby, the only familiar object, driving exactly the same rig he had in the early sixties."

Of course the man's impression of the rig was incorrect, although the style and color of the turnout never changed.

Once I interviewed the old gentleman. It was near the close of his life. Among other things he told me the following incidents:

"Along in the late fifties Miss Ann Purdy came from Syracuse to Banksville. She bought the house opposite the post office, considerably enlarged it and established a boarding school for girls and boys. Much to the surprise of everyone in Banksville she soon had a houseful and roomed a few outside.

"At that time there was no regular communication with the village and she induced me to start the Banksville and Greenwich stage line. She lent me one hundred dollars and I made my first trip June

23, 1861. For many years I carried ten passengers daily. The pupils and teachers patronized me freely and even after the school was abandoned, way down into the seventies, the business was pretty good.

THE STANWICH CHURCH. SHUBEL BRUSH HOME-
STEAD IN THE BACKGROUND
Photo by J. C. Bonnett

"My line was a feeder to the steamer *John Romer* and the president, Sanford Mead, always passed me to New York and back, but I seldom went. In those days the members of the Americus Club often hired me to drive them to Rye Beach or Stamford and many times I had Boss Tweed with me on the front seat.

"I left Banksville at six o'clock, caught the *Romer*

[63]

at seven and left my railroad passengers for the 7.21
train. This gave me all day in the village, as I did
not leave on the return trip until the arrival of the
steamer at about six o'clock.

"But business isn't what it once was and sometimes

WILLIAM BRUSH HOMESTEAD
Stanwich
Photo by J. C. Bonnett

on the up trip the hills seem steeper and longer than
they once did and the horses seem to pull with a
greater effort. Then it is that I realize that the
whole rig from the driver down is getting old and
that the best of life lies far, far behind."

South of Banksville lies Stanwich, even more
quaint than its sister village. It had a country store
that was closed when the rural free delivery drove

out the postoffice, but there still remains an old inn, now used as a dwelling and a beautiful country church, built in the latter part of the eighteenth century.

Its graceful white spire first comes in view as one drives north by Rockwood Lake. The wide shingles that cover it are hand wrought and its large windows are glazed with diminutive panes. What a crime it would be to supplant those ancient lights with modern stained glass windows!

A beautiful stained glass window is a joy forever, provided it is correctly placed. Such a window in a country church, which nestles among trees, or is shadowed by mountains, or commands a broad prospect of hill and dale, is an intrusion. But in a city church among brick walls, the beauty of stained glass takes the place of nature's decoration, and helps the worshiper to forget the sordid world about him.

In this connection I must quote from the Right Rev. William Lawrence, the Bishop of Massachusetts. Recently he spoke of the rededication of the old North Church in Boston—the ancient house of worship from whose belfry the lanterns are said to have shone forth which guided Paul Revere on his famous ride:

"Fortunately no stained glass has ever desecrated these windows. No painted glass can give greater beauty than the sky and the swinging branches of the trees seen through the transparent panes of a Colonial church."

[65]

OTHER DAYS IN GREENWICH

Everything about the church, inside and out, is consistent with its age. It rests peacefully under the shadow of great trees that have afforded comfort and delight to several generations.

In other days much of this territory belonged to Charles, William and Shubel Brush, with the Ingersols also appearing as land owners.

Many of the Stanwich people were interested in tanning, Shubel Brush being the last to engage in it. He lived on the corner, back of the church in an ancient house, which since his death has been much changed architecturally.

His brother, William, lived on the cross road in an antique mansion now included within the bounds of Semloh farm. Reverse the spelling and you have the owner's name.

The little village of Stanwich is suggestive of bygone days, when the stagecoach to Bedford made a stop at the old Inn. That building is now owned by Mrs. A. Leta Bonnett, of New Haven, and Harriette L. Lockwood, granddaughters of Shubel Brush. It presents a story of the long ago in its sweeping roof and quaint windows.

Within, its wide fireplaces, in each room, and its brick oven suggest the near-by forest, with its ample supply of wood. The second floor was designed for a ball room and as occasion required, the partitions were hooked to the ceiling and the young people, with their friends from Bedford, and North Castle, made merry all the night long.

BANKSVILLE AND STANWICH

Stories are told of a flourishing boys' boarding school on the west road kept by Theodore June.

There were debating clubs in the olden days of which there are many traditions and a few stray records.

Sometimes I have heard this hamlet called East Stanwich. The old records give the name of Stanwich to all the territory below Banksville, extending east as far as "the Farms" in Stamford Township.

The direct road from the Borough to Bedford through Stanwich has always been known as "the west street."

There seems to be no reason for applying the name of East Stanwich to what is now and has always been the center of Stanwich.

OLD INN AT STANWICH
Photo by J. C. Bonnett

CHAPTER VI

JUST at this point I must write of the Davis' Dock, over which there has been much litigation, and the ownership of which is still misunderstood. At a town meeting held in Greenwich, June 15, 1716, the following resolution was adopted. It has generally been known as the Justus Bush grant and I give it exactly as it appears in the Common place book in our Land Records.

"The Towne by vot do give & grant unto Mr. "Justice Bush of New York the privilege of the "stream of horseneck brook below the country road to "build a grist mill or mills upon & sd Justice Bush "is to build said mill within two years time from this "date & to grind for the inhabitants of Green- "wich what grain they shall bring to his mill to be "ground & not to put them by for strangers & he is "to have liberty to gett stones & timber upon com- "mon lands for buildings and mill & also to sett up "a store house upon said landing, & said Justice "Bush is constantly to maintain a sufficient grist mill "upon sd stream, except said mill should come to "some accident by fire or otherwise, & said Justice

[68]

THE DAVIS DOCK

"Bush do not rebuild her again within three years
"time then the said stream & privileges to return for
"their use and benefit as formerly; and further Mr.
"Ebenezer Mead & Angel Husted & John Ferris are
"chosen to lay out the landing and highway on the
"north side of Horseneck brook."

What did this grant mean? Was the mill to be
built on town property or on the Bush property, the
grant applying only to the use of the brook which
Mr. Bush had under his title to the shore of the
stream? The Davis family, who succeeded the Bush
ownership, always supposed they owned the fee of the
land and for many generations they paid the town
taxes thereon.

In 1837 considerable contention arose over this
property, which then included a dock as well as a
mill. But the only question was as to whether it was
a public or private dock. The distinction is wholly
as to whether wharfage has been charged or not. A
private dock may be maintained upon one's own
shore front but when the owner accepts wharfage it
immediately becomes a public dock to which any vessel may tie upon the due tender of wharfage.

After the death of Eleanor R. Davis this property
belonged, under her will, to Mrs. Amelia J. Dougan
and an action was tried in the Court of Common
Pleas between Mrs. Dougan and the town to determine her rights therein.

It seems from the decision of the Court of Errors,
to which the case went for final determination, that

after the litigation was over the question of the ownership of the land was still undetermined.

There was a tradition that the same question had once before been tried and considerable time and money were expended in an effort to find the old files.

Finally, after the Dougan case was disposed of the papers were discovered among the criminal files, stored in the garret of the County Court House in Bridgeport. These files disclosed the fact that in 1837 the question as to whether the dock was public or private was determined in favor of Walter Davis then the owner.

Capt. Charles Studwell, a boat owner, assumed to use the dock without paying Mr. Davis wharfage and thereupon he brought suit claiming $30 damages. The case was tried before Ephraim Golden, a justice of the peace, and the hearing began September 12, 1837, at the Inn of Benjamin Page at Mianus Landing.

Jacob Dayton, Jr., was the constable who served the papers and his fees were taxed at ninety-four cents.

After due hearing, the Court, on October 11, rendered a judgment for $8.00 for the plaintiff, Walter Davis, with his costs taxed at $10.41, and an appeal was taken to the County Court.

This suit was remarkable for the personnel of the Counsel engaged.

Charles Hawley, of Stamford, one of the most

eminent lawyers of the State, signed the writ. He appeared in the Page Inn at Mianus and tried and won the suit for Mr. Davis.

Associated with him was the famous Roger Minot Sherman, who, shortly after the trial of the case, became a judge of the Supreme Court. He died in Fairfield in 1844.

The trial of the case created intense excitement in town and was the subject of much discussion for years afterward. Capt. Studwell, being defeated, appealed through his counsel, Joshua B. Ferris, of Stamford, then a youth, to the County Court (since abolished) where the case was tried before a jury consisting of Walter Sherwood, Stephen Raymond, Moses Birkly, Jr., Christopher Hubbel, Benjamin C. Smith, Samuel Beardsley, William B. Dyer, Horace Waterbury, John Holmes, Isaac Scofield, Noah Knapp and John Young. The trial occurred in Fairfield, then the County Seat, in April, 1839, and resulted in a judgment for Mr. Davis. An arrest of judgment was filed and final judgment was not entered until May 18, 1840.

The witnesses who appeared before the Justice at Mianus and before the County Court were Silas Davis, a son of the plaintiff, B. Morrell, M. Mead, J. L. Bush, William Hubbard, Joseph Brush, Paul Ferris and Samuel Ferris. After this, the Davises, for several generations, continued to collect wharfage. In Mrs. Dougan's case, referred to above, the Supreme Court of Errors decided that the dock was a public dock but the question of the ownership of the land was not determined. The case is reported in 77 Con. Rep., page 444.

In terminating the opinion written by Judge Hall, the Court says: "The answer does not allege ownership in the town but that the locus [the place] was a public dock and landing place."

CHAPTER VII

RECURRING again to the centrally-located farms as outlined in the beginning of Chapter I, I desire herein to include in one description the farms of Thomas A. Mead and Zaccheus Mead.

These two farms, divided by the Glenville road, comprising three or four hundred acres, stretched away from the Post Road, in valley and hill to the north and west, ending in woodland.

The Thomas A. Mead homestead was built in 1799 by Richard Mead and is known as *Dearfield*. The name is not misspelled but has a significant meaning. Various stories are told of its derivation: the one most likely to be true is as follows: One of Richard Mead's family, in writing to a friend, described the fields of waving grain through the valleys, along the knolls and ridges to the "Hemlock Woods"; all visible from the windows of the house and characterizes them as "dear fields."

Dearfield Drive takes its name from the same incident.

The Thomas A. Mead farm is now known as Edgewood Park, and the Zaccheus Mead farm as Rock Ridge.

[73]

Fifty years ago looking north from the Post Road at all that great acreage, the two farms seemed one. There were plowed fields, waving grain and rock-ribbed hills, while to the west the beautiful Hemlock Woods always took the last rays of the setting sun.

The Zaccheus Mead homestead, lately the home of

"DEARFIELDS"
Thos. A. Mead Homestead
Built 1799

Charles B. Read, deceased, stood out all alone, prominent against the northern sky. In all that great stretch from the Post Road to the woods at the north and west, there was scarcely a tree, excepting two or three apple orchards and the small wood lot near the residence of Judge Charles D. Burnes on Brookside Drive.

Farmers always were solicitous for their lands

under cultivation and a shaded field was usually un-productive. But I recall how desolate that old Zaccheus Mead homestead looked standing all alone against the steely gray winter sky.

From the same point of view it is now lost in a

THOMAS A. MEAD
1799-1892

jungle of shade trees or by the obstruction of inter-vening buildings.

This great territory was divided by ancient stone walls, thick and straight and frequently intersected by other similar walls. These walls were made of boulders that could be drawn only by four pair of oxen and lifted to their place by a derrick. Walls were thus frequent because of the supply of stone dug from the earth to make the cultivated fields.

Not far from the Edgewood Inn, which, with the Park of the same name, occupies a small portion of the Thomas A. Mead farm, one may still see a few examples of the wall-building skill of the generation that lived before and just after the Revolution. There are still remaining short pieces of old walls, covered with moss and vines, so wide that a horse and buggy could be driven along the top. But most of the old walls have been broken to pieces and are occupying their place in modern house construction.

The old homestead at Rock Ridge was owned and occupied by two men of the same name—Zaccheus Mead. The first was the grandfather of the second, but I have no knowledge of the generation between, except that Job and Elsie were the parents of Zaccheus.

However, the old homestead and its one hundred and fifty acres went, by will, from grandfather to grandson of the same name.

Opposite the "Boulders" now the home of E. B. Close, the rock caverns of that jagged granite pile, rising more than fifty feet in height, afforded a safe hiding place, when the British red coats made life uncomfortable for the Greenwich patriots. There was no road near there when I was a boy, but one day, going through those woods in company with my

father and Col. Thomas, as Mr. Mead was almost
always called, the latter pointed out the rocks as the
hiding place of refugees during the war. It wasn't
quite clear to me what was meant by refugees but
the words sounded spookish, and the surrounding
dense woods, with the murmur of Horseneck Brook,

ZACCHEUS MEAD HOMESTEAD
In 1859

were not agreeable to my nerves and I never go
through there without recalling the incident. The
brook is the same and so are the trees and rocks but
the human habitations have taken away all the somber mystery of my first visit.

It is possible that the old homestead still standing
supplanted one earlier built, but I am inclined to be-

lieve that the first one, an old sweep-back, was probably enlarged and improved, thus creating the present building. But whether so or not the present house is the oldest in Rock Ridge.

Inside I believe it is appropriately furnished in antique and certainly with much more luxury than was enjoyed by either of its former occupants.

The first Zaccheus was an old man when he died, October 27, 1846. Having lived all his life in the old place he had gathered about him a few Windsor chairs, as well as some straight back rush bottoms, and on a winter night, when the great open fireplace was the only means of heating the living room, the big high-backed settle was the most comfortable spot in which to crack nuts, eat apples or drink cider before the cheerful fire.

If some of the Rock Ridge folks could see the house as it was then, how they would wax enthusiastic over the ancient high-posted and canopied beds, the mahogany tables and brass warming pans; the blue dishes in the corner cupboards and all those quaint and lowly things that made the Colonial housekeeper contented and happy. He had all these things because they and many more articles are enumerated in the inventory of his estate. Beyond these simple articles of personal property he had nothing but the wagon, the pung and the chaise.

Zaccheus made his will on the 15th day of April, 1833,—thirteen years before his death. And thereby the old farm went to the grandson, Zaccheus, subject

[78]

to the life use of one-third by the widow. Her name was Deborah and she continued to enjoy her life estate until September 8, 1853.

The old man gave Deborah only the use of one-

ZACCHEUS MEAD 2ND
1798-1872

third of the farm and the buildings and he must have strained a point in his conception of the law of dower when he gave her the unrestricted use of all his household furniture "except the clock and birch bedstead and bed and bedding and warming pan." The clock was a tall one that stood in the living room while the banjo clock that hung in the hall was called the time-piece.

What has become of all those interesting old relics? They must have remained in the homestead many years, but I imagine that finally when the clock and the timepiece, in the days of a later generation refused to go, they were discarded for modern ones on the theory that they were old and all worn out. I think the second Zaccheus must have kept them, because as I recall him, during war times, he was just such an old-fashioned man as would hold on to the goods of his ancestors. He was accustomed to drive along the dusty road every Sunday in his antique wagon drawn by a fat and logy gray horse, headed for the Second Congregational Church, where he stayed till the close of the afternoon service at three o'clock. His wife and his only child, Hannah R. Mead, were always with him.

Many are still living who recall with interest the members of this quaint family.

Hannah came into possession of the farm in the spring of 1872 and there she and her mother lived, honored and respected by all who knew them.

Hannah died in 1882 and her mother, Laura Mead, continued to live in the old homestead until January 13, 1895. Although she outlived her daughter so many years she was kindly cared for by Nathaniel Witherell who supplied her with every comfort in her last days.

Why Nathaniel Witherell?

[80]

Nathaniel Witherell

1841–1906

ROCKRIDGE AND DEARFIELD

Hannah R. Mead was a very benevolent woman. In her last will she gave legacy after legacy to benevolent societies and institutions of learning. While she reserved to her mother a life estate, there was practically nothing left but the old homestead and the farm. The old lady could scarcely be expected to get a living and pay her taxes from the sale of produce. That day had passed.

As I look over Rock Ridge and note its beautiful villas, its fine lawns and productive gardens, it is hard to realize that less than twenty-five years ago the whole place was solemnly appraised at twelve thousand dollars. And what is still more remarkable, that appraisal is three thousand dollars less than it was after the death of the first Zaccheus in 1846.

I am not criticizing the appraisers but only pointing out the fact that two generations ago our farms had a greater value than they had a generation ago, because the value was estimated on their productiveness. In 1846 they were making their owners rich. Did you ever notice the old potato cellar on Round Island and on many of the way back farms?

In 1872 all this was changed. The great west had used up the eastern farmer and farms were hardly salable. Now that is all changed again. The automobile has made the distant farm available and the fruit-grower has discovered that the New England apple is the best of all.

The farm being in the market, Mr. Witherell bought it with the widow's life estate remaining.

This is how he got it. Everybody, especially, a missionary society or a struggling college, is looking for the present rather than the future dollar. And a long list of quit-claim deeds from all the beneficiaries under Hannah R. Mead's will shows how the title passed. It was an uncertainty how long the life tenant would be an encumbrance, but three years before her death Mr. Witherell gathered in all the shares and became the owner.

And how fortunate for the old lady that he did, for while the various benevolent societies were conducting their operations in foreign lands they might not have been so attentive to the aged life tenant at Rock Ridge as was Mr. Witherell.

The records are silent as to the cost of Rock Ridge but I have it on very good authority that it was $14,500.

The roads and avenues were laid out, sewer and water pipes introduced and when the park was all completed three acre plots sold for $15,000.

Such transactions as this account for the remarkable growth of Greenwich.

In 1872 the Zaccheus Mead farm was assessed at $12,000, but now Rock Ridge, with all its improvements, pays taxes on an assessment fifty times greater than that insignificant amount.

Not long after Mr. Witherell came to Greenwich he opened a Fresh Air Home for children at Indian Field. At that time the Isaac Howe Mead homestead was standing, and here he located "The Fold," as the home was called. But he discovered that no facilities for obtaining water existed, and for this reason he moved "The Fold" to Rock Ridge. It was located on the cedar knoll now occupied by William F. Decker's handsome bungalow. Not less than two hundred children were cared for at one time.

In a house nearby called "Cherryvale," owned by Mr. Witherell, for six consecutive seasons the Working Girls' Vacation Society of New York gave healthful rest and recreation to the hard working girls, thirty-five at a time.

As the town grew these institutions were found to be too near the village, and their abandonment was deemed advisable.

CHAPTER VIII

THE farms lying to the east of the village belonged to Theodore H. Mead, Philander Button and Titus Mead. The Titus Mead farm will be
considered later and an allusion to the Button farm
is included in one of the chapters devoted to William
M. Tweed.

The Theodore H. Mead farm consisted of sixty-
five acres, according to the record, but was actually
about eighty acres in extent. It included the ancient
house at the foot of Putnam Hill, now owned by
John Maher. It was from the front porch of this
house, in the early morning of February 26, 1779,
that Gen. Ebenezer Mead saw Gen. Putnam make
his famous escape from the British dragoons. It
was the General's grandson, Theodore, who owned
and occupied the house when I first saw it.

It is difficult now to realize that in 1859 Theodore
H. Mead was only thirty-seven years old and that
when he died, January 18, 1876, he was but fifty-four
years old. He always seemed an elderly man, owing
perhaps to the fact that my eyes were youthful and
also to the peculiar mode of dress adopted by Mr.
Mead. He always wore a slouch hat, a shirt that

[86]

was decidedly negligee and trousers thrust into the tops of boots that were never blacked. He rarely wore a coat. He had the habit of riding to the village for his mail, without a saddle and often without a bridle. There was nothing about the man or about his farm suggestive of tidiness. The bars were generally down and his cattle out.

And yet, notwithstanding these defects, he was a man well born and well schooled. He was proud of his ancestry and of the fact that he was born in the old homestead at the foot of Putnam Hill that had housed his warrior grandsire. His wife was the daughter of Rev. William Cooper Mead, D.D., LL.D., of Norwalk, an eminent divine well known throughout New England.

His father married twice and he was the youngest of eleven children. He had a half-brother, Rev. Ebenezer Mead, who was a Congregational minister.

He often expressed the regret that his father was not able to afford him a liberal and professional education. He died in the same room in which he was born.

He had converted the ten acre meadow into a pond, since known as "Ten Acres," splendid for skating but used for the purpose of gathering ice and for many years he alone dealt in it. Just east of the homestead was a mill site, still extant, which afforded excellent water power by which a saw mill and cider mill were in commission all the year round. It is only a few years ago that the mill was removed but the pond remains an ornament to the Milton C. Nichols place, recently erected near it.

Giving attention to the mill and ice crop explained in part why the farm was not more carefully cultivated. Furthermore his sixty-five acres included considerable woodland from which wood was carted to various people about the village and in Cos Cob. The balance, devoted to cultivation, was probably no more than enough to maintain his oxen, a few cows, sheep and a pair of horses.

Another reason for the lack of attention given to the farm and mill was Mr. Mead's growing passion for speculation.

He was always in a hurry to get rich and followed the gold market with a vigilant eye. During the war of 1861 and up to 1879 gold was at a premium over currency which necessitated its purchase in the open market when required for mercantile purposes or the payment of customs duties. The gold board in New York city, as the exchange was called, was opened to trade in gold coin, just as stocks are in the regular exchange.

Frequently gold fluctuated rapidly and many countrymen, like Mr. Mead, were interested in buying and selling for a quick profit. He was therefore always a borrower and constantly in trouble with small local creditors. A large number of attachments were filed against his farm and sometimes judgments were entered against him. This condition of affairs arose from his inattention to business and not because he desired to ignore the demands of creditors. Whenever he was sued he took it as a matter of course, paid the costs, treated the sheriff to a glass of cider and repeated the operation two or three times within the next week.

Volume 39 of the land records devoted to real estate attachments tells the full story of Theodore's troubles, though perhaps I ought not to characterize them thus for Mr. Mead rarely was troubled with anything.

He liked children, perhaps because he had none of his own. When the Cos Cob boys, students at the Academy, came up the hill by the mill—a very steep hill that long ago disappeared under modern grading and road making—he would often call them in and removing the bung of a barrel filled with sweet cider supply them with the necessary straws. If the cider was running through the spout from the press he would hand them a tin cup with which to drink their fill. In winter these same boys and many others helped to float the ice cakes down to the slide.

On one occasion Mr. Mead was invited to attend the annual dinner of the New England Society in the City of New York and promptly accepted.

He went with my father and I then realized that Theodore H. Mead, dressed in dark clothes, with polished boots and a silk hat, was a very handsome man. Once riding along on a bay nag that seemed too frail to carry him, he drew up in front of the Academy, then on the corner where Dr. F. C. Hyde's house stands, while the boys were enjoying the noon recess. Calling us around him he told the story of Putnam's ride giving it to us just as he had heard it from the lips of his grandfather, an eye witness.

When Mr. Mead died his creditors were numerous and eventually his estate was settled as an insolvent estate.

Col. Thomas A. Mead had loaned him ten thousand dollars made up of various small sums and his appeal from the commissioners on Theodore's estate furnishes some law, still unrevoked. It is only necessary for me to refer to the 46 Vol. of Conn. Reports, page 417, and to suggest that if the details of a financial wreck are interesting they may there be found.

I started to tell about the farm but have devoted most of the chapter to its eccentric owner.

The estate being insolvent all of the farm was sold at auction by order of the Court of Probate. It was a rainy morning in the spring of 1881, and yet there was a good deal of money in the crowd that gathered about the auctioneer, in front of the old homestead. The sixty-five acres, with ice house, mill right, barns and the grand old Colonial house, brought only $5,400, less than $100 an acre. The widow, Cornelia J. Mead, was then living and as the property was sold subject to her dower it had an influence to depress the price.

Subsequently, Solomon Mead, John Dayton and Allen H. Close, as distributors appointed by the court, set out to her the use for life of the house and about four acres of land.

She died on the 26th day of October, 1881. The property went to Henry Webb and afterwards to John Maher and much of their fortune may be traced to that fortunate purchase on that rainy spring morning in 1881. If you ask the genial ice and coal dealer, John Maher, how much he has made out of

BUTTERMILK FALLS
Photo by I. L. Mead

the farm he will respond with a jolly laugh and nothing more. The small parcel recently sold is said to have brought $20,000.

The farm included a large tract on the south side of the road now included in Milbank and the famous and romantic Buttermilk Falls tract on the north. Here are the homes of E. Belcher Mead and J. M. Menendez, with rustic ledges, beautiful trees, the ever murmuring brook and the view of Long Island Sound.

[91]

CHAPTER IX

THE TITUS MEAD FARM

EVERY one knows Titus Mead's hill. It is one of the old names that still remain. It is appropriate, for at its crest, for many years lived a farmer of that name. The line of splendid maple trees along the road side was planted by him nearly ninety years ago.

He died March 26, 1869, at the age of sixty-five years. By him were built some of the stone walls that divide the fields and many of the drains that have made the land so fertile. He was prominent in town affairs, when I was a boy, and for many years was Town Treasurer.

His wife was Lucy Mumford Mead, daughter of Andrew Mead, who died April 21, 1821, "a patriot of the Revolution," according to his epitaph.

Titus Mead was one of the wealthy men of his time. He had a large and profitable farm, with a short haul to the market sloops. The inventory of his estate reveals only the choicest securities and a long list of local mortgages.

He was a liberal man. As the treasurer of a certain lodge, in the village it was said that he always paid the bills although they were far in excess of the receipts for which he was always unanimously re-elected.

He wrote his own will, using a printed blank in which it was necessary only to insert the name of his wife as sole legatee and devisee. He executed it July 9, 1862, which fact would appear of no moment except that the names of the subscribing

TITUS MEAD HOMESTEAD
In 1859

witnesses bring back to me a vivid recollection of an old wheelwright's shop shaded by a mammoth button-ball tree which stood where the First Presbyterian Church now stands. Joseph E. Russell ran the shop and George S. Ray worked for him. Samuel Close, the Town Clerk and Justice of the Peace, had his office near-by. This office is fully described in Chapter III of this volume.

These three men witnessed the execution of the will and we can readily imagine Squire Close calling the other two to come across to his little office, while the

shop was left alone, without danger of anyone calling during those dull days.

Titus Mead's widow outlived him twenty-two
years and many of her personal friends survive her.
She was a delightful lady of the old school and it
always gave me the greatest pleasure to call upon her.
The year after her husband's death, in 1870, she
built the house on lower North Street since very
much enlarged by the late
H. P. Whittaker, and
now belonging to his es-
tate. He called the place
Prescourt.

MRS. LUCY MUMFORD MEAD
1810-1891

Living in the village
was much more to her
taste, than living in the
old farmhouse at the top
of the hill, after her husband had gone. But she
thought a great deal of
the place and although she had many offers she would
not part with it. She did, however, sell many acres of
her farm, including Crest View to Henry C. Boswell,
and the William H. Teed and Thomas Young tracts.

"The Chimneys" and "Athelcroft" were built by
Clarence M. Hyde and his late brother on a portion of
Mrs. Mead's farm. It became the good fortune later
of Mrs. Mary E. Andrews to purchase from the Lucy
M. Mead estate the valuable tract upon which stands
the fine house built by her and since her decease

[94]

owned by her daughter, Mrs. F. Kissam Brown. She also owns the old Titus Mead homestead and she and her husband have shown their wisdom and good taste in retaining the old house much as it appeared, in the days that followed the Revolution when it was one of the mansions of the town.

Adjoining the Titus Mead farm on the south lies

PUTNAM COTTAGE
The home for nearly a century of Hezekiah and John J.
Tracy, father and son

territory that has an interesting Revolutionary history.

In 1775 Israel Knapp lived in what is now known as Putnam cottage. He also owned many acres in the neighborhood of "Great Hill" as it was called before Putnam's exploit. Dying without a will his land descended to his widow and heirs who subsequently sold it to Reuben Holmes. He was a man of character, education and standing; by profession a teacher, by trade a shoemaker. He had a large

[95]

family and their support taxed his abilities to the ut-
most. In his school by day, he sat on his bench at
night and was not satisfied if he failed to finish half
a dozen pair of shoes weekly.

But finally he abandoned the struggle, sold his real
estate August 16, 1823, and moved to what was then
the far west, Geneva, Cayuga County, New York.
Mrs. Hannah Mead bought the property consisting
of thirty-two acres, for $3,500. She was the widow
of Joshua Mead who died early in life leaving an
only child, Solomon, so well known to the present
generation. This parcel of land extended north and
included land now owned by the Parmelee J. McFadden estate.

One of the daughters of Israel Knapp was Amy
K. Thompson, who appears to have retained an interest in her father's land and upon her decease her
four children, Harriet, Cornelia, James and Caroline,
conveyed it to Solomon Mead's mother.

Mr. Mead always spoke of his mother with great
admiration and affection and all her transactions indi-
cate that she was a woman of unusual ability. She
died March 14, 1844, at the age of 79, leaving Solomon as her sole heir at law.

Solomon Mead was a prominent man in Greenwich
all his life and at his decease June 14, 1898, it was
found that he was worth more than any other native
of the town who had passed his days here.

He was an intelligent, practical and painstaking
man. While his mother owned the little farm of

[96]

thirty-one acres, which she never encumbered, he made many improvements upon the property. The blind ditches he laid for drainage purposes still re-

Solomon Mead

1808–1898

main to attest his skillful, scientific handling of the property.

Its present appearance, due to change in fence lines, opening of highways, demolition of old buildings, the erection of new ones, and the planting of fruit and ornamental trees—is very different from its appearance eighty years ago.

Long before my remembrance an old house and a barn stood near the highway between the present Whittaker and McFadden places. Not many years ago I found the old well near the present line of highway in front of the old cellar hole. These old buildings are immortalized in Daniel Merritt Mead's history of Greenwich, pages 156, 157 and 158.

After the tenancy of the Holmes family in the Putnam cottage it was owned and occupied by Hezekiah and John Jay Tracy, father and son, for nearly a century. They were both men of attainments and they each occupied the office of Town Clerk for many years. John Jay was secretary of the Tammany Society in New York. The public records kept by these men are models of penmanship at a time when a quill pen only was used.

For many years the street running near the Putnam cottage through land of A. Foster Higgins was appropriately called Tracy Street. Its present name of Park Avenue has no particular significance.

Prior to 1858 Solomon Mead lived in an old fashioned sweep-back, standing just inside the gateway leading to the stone mansion erected by him in 1854-1858. The house is known as No. 48 Maple Avenue and has recently been occupied by the family of William Cooney. After the completion of the new residence, in 1859, the old one was removed. It was a prototype of the old Jared Mead house, described in Chapter XIV. Under its front windows were bunches of phlox and some marigolds were nodding in the summer breeze when I first saw it. It had a comfortable "sit down" appearance, characteristic of all the old gray shingle, low studded sweep-backs of the eighteenth century. Near its north end was the well house in which an empty bucket hung over the curb. It was overshadowed by the great stone house which was then completed, and it was only a short time afterward that it disappeared and the old cellar hole was filled.

Mr. Mead began to build the present stone house in 1854 and completed it in 1858. The method of thorough construction adopted by its owner attracted wide attention. The walls were hollow to prevent dampness and the stones were laid up in shell lime.

Mr. Mead has often told me that in those days, from his front piazza, he enjoyed an unobstructed view of Long Island Sound as far east as the Norwalk Islands. But in late years the shade trees growing tall and rank have destroyed much of the summer view.

CHAPTER X

O N November 9, 1916, will occur the two hundredth anniversary of the establishment of the Second Congregational Church. The one hundred and fiftieth anniversary was held in 1866 and was one of the most important that ever occurred in Greenwich. A similar occasion in these days would cause less interest outside the church membership, because the population is larger, more varied in religious faith, and perhaps more secular in disposition. But the celebration in 1866 was largely attended and created among the members of all religious sects a general interest.

The present stone church, a creation of Leopold Eidlitz, one of the most famous church architects of the Nineteenth century, arouses the admiration of every resident of Greenwich, whatever his creed or nationality.

It was built in 1856 under somewhat peculiar circumstances. Its predecessors had been comparatively cheap, wooden affairs and when the building of a new church was agitated Mr. Robert Williams Mead led the minority in advocating the construction of the present building. Not only plans but a perfect model in plaster were shown, displaying the splendid proportions and lines of the proposed church.

ROBERT W. MEAD
1814-1875

The proposition was strongly opposed on the ground of expense, but finally when Mr. Mead declared it could be built for thirty thousand dollars someone at the church meeting expressed a doubt as to his ability to find a contractor to undertake the work at that price. It is not unlikely that Mr. Mead

[101]

realized this, for he promptly replied that he would take the contract himself.

He was not a contractor and never had been one, but he built the church and when the thirty thousand dollar appropriation was exhausted he sold his own securities to continue and complete the building.

His monument stands near the church and bears the same inscription that is cut in the tomb of Sir Christopher Wren in St. Pauls, London, *"Si monumentum quarae circumspice"*—"If you would see his monument look about."

I fear that Robert Williams Mead never received half the credit that should have been his for building the handsomest church spire in New England.

He was a son of Dr. Darius Mead, whose home was on the crest of Putnam Hill. He had made a fortune in mercantile pursuits in New York City. When he built the church he resided in the house now owned and occupied by his nephew, Frederick Mead. On April 11, 1864, he sold this property to D. Jackson Steward, who held it till April 15, 1868, when he sold it to Edward Slosson, a retired New York lawyer. Mrs. Annie Turnbull Slosson, his widow, a well-known writer, now resides in New York. After the death of Mr. Slosson, by a deed dated May 28, 1872, the property went to Frederick Mead, the father of its present owner.

The interior of the church was remodeled in 1900, at an expense of about thirty thousand dollars. Those who had the matter in hand probably acted

2ND CONGREGATIONAL CHURCH IN 1879
(No clock at that time)
Pastors: Rev. Dr. Joel H. Linsley, Rev. Dr. Frederick G. Clark,
Rev. Dr. George A. Gordon

for the best interests of the church. However, such a radical change was a great disappointment to me.

There is one incident in connection with the building of this church that should not be omitted. When it was fully completed with the outside scaffolding still surrounding the spire several ladies, members of the church, climbed on open ladders, from scaffold to scaffold, till they reached the circular cap stone, eight feet in diameter, around which they sat and ate their supper, undisturbed by the fact that they were two hundred and twelve feet above the ground. Mrs. Julia A. Button, Miss Clarissa Mead and Mrs. Edward Mead were among the number.

But to recur to the celebration of 1866. It comes back to me like an occurrence of yesterday. Perhaps its most remarkable feature was the historical address by Rev. Joel H. Linsley, D.D., which was his last public effort. He had been the pastor of the church for nineteen years and was then the honorary but retired pastor. His address, finished and scholarly, was replete with matters of local history and startling in its prophetic portrayal of the speaker's vision of the future, in these words.

"This town will not for many years, if ever, be a place distinguished for business or rapid advance in population. On this very account it is all the better for a place of quiet homes, and as a seat for the best educational institutions."

The committee of arrangements consisted of Deacon Philander Button, Deacon Jonas Mead, Dr. T.

S. Pinneo, William A. Howe and Edward P. Holly. They were appointed at a meeting of the church held in March, 1866.

During the summer the work of arranging details became so onerous that the committee was enlarged by adding the following men: Isaac L. Mead, Alexander Mead, Zophar Mead, Shadrach M. Brush, Benjamin Wright, Arthur D. Mead, George H. Mills, Gideon Reynolds and the following ladies: Mrs. Edward Mead, Mrs. Philander Button, Mrs. T. S. Pinneo, Mrs. Joseph Brush, Mrs. Augustus N. Reynolds, Mrs. Benjamin Wright, Mrs. Elizabeth S. Hoyt, Mrs. Stephen Holly, Mrs. Moses Cristy, Mrs. Nehemiah Howe, Mrs. Daniel Merritt Mead, Mrs. Charles H. Seaman, Mrs. William B. Sherwood, Mrs. Thomas Ritch, Mrs. Lockwood P. Clark, Mrs. Caleb Holmes, Mrs. Alfred Bell, Mrs. Isaac Peck, Mrs. Jabez Mead, Mrs. Stephen G. White, Mrs. Henry M. Bailey, Mrs. William T. Reynolds, Mrs. Lewis A. Merritt, Miss Hannah M. Mead, Miss Eliza J. Scofield, Mrs. Joseph E. Russell, Miss Louisa Mead.

As I write these names their owners' faces all come back to me. Of the committee of men four survive and but one of the committee of women is living.

The day was one of the finest of the season. It was one of those glorious autumn days for which Greenwich has always been so famous and when doubt often arises whether there is more beauty in the blue waters of the Sound or in the wealth of forest trees, flaming with scarlet and orange.

The church was decorated with festoons and wreaths of evergreen, tastefully interwoven with autumn flowers. Upon the wall over the speakers' platform, in the rear of where the organ now stands was the following inscription:

IN THE PLACE OF THE FATHERS ARE THE CHILDREN

1716

OUR FATHER'S GOD IS OUR GOD

The printed programme, a copy of which lies before me, announced the following order of exercises.

1. *Invocation*   REV. PLATT T. HOLLY
2. *Reading the Scriptures*   REV. F. G. CLARK, D.D.
3. *Anthem*—"O, How Lovely is Zion."
4. *Prayer*   REV. JOEL MANN
5. *Historical Discourse*   REV. J. H. LINSLEY, D.D.
6. *Prayer*   REV. SAMUEL HOWE
7. *Anthem*—"Praise Ye the Lord."
8. *Benediction*   REV. STEPHEN HUBBELL

RECESS FOR COLLATION

P. M.

9. *Anthem.*
10. *Welcoming Address*   REV. W. H. H. MURRAY
11. *Historical Paper*   WILLIAM A. HOWE
12. *Anthem.* .. ..
13. *History Stillson Benevolent Society*
                            DR. T. S. PINNEO

Would it be possible in this generation to hold an audience on such an occasion all day long?

OTHER DAYS IN GREENWICH

The historical address, as I have stated, was the crowning effort of Dr. Linsley's busy life. He died March 22, 1868. It may not be amiss to quote here the peroration of that discourse.

"This is, my hearers, of all the days since Feaks and Patrick cut the waves of the Sound with their light boat, fastened her to Elizabeth Neck, and by peaceful purchase took possession of these fair fields for civilized man, the best and brightest, the one in which it is the greatest privilege to live.

"That our children and children's children are to see a still brighter one, I hope, nay, I believe.

"And when we scatter at the close of this auspicious occasion from this beloved hill of Zion, let us retire with gratitude for what our fathers bequeathed to us from the past; with rejoicing in the present, that the lines have fallen to us in pleasant places, and with full purpose of heart, that, God helping us, we will transmit a still richer inheritance to those who shall come after us, even to the latest generations."

The afternoon session opened with an address of welcome by Rev. W. H. H. Murray which seemed to be particularly directed to the ministers present who had formerly been pastors of the church.

Mr. Murray was at that time a young man of twenty-six years and acting pastor of the church. To most of the guests he was unknown, but the address of welcome thrilled every soul and left such an impression that the memory of Murray was never dimmed.

I recall distinctly, how in the midst of his address, he ran his fingers through his thick, raven locks and, turning his massive figure towards Rev. Joel Mann, the oldest ex-pastor, said: "But more especially do we rejoice that you, the most aged of this group, whose sun, though glowing and bright, is near the border of the horizon, should once more be with us, to behold and be made happy at the sight of our prosperity, before the shadows deepen farther, and you, passing through them, be lost to our eyes.

"It is well, too, that those of us in this congregation whose heads, in the passage of years, have whitened with yours, should see once more the familiar faces, the countenances of former and still beloved pastors, before that hand, which smites the cloud for all, smites it asunder for us, and our eyes close on terrestrial objects forever."

I think the most touching incident of the day occurred at its close, when Mr. Murray rose and said: "There is one man, my good friends, who did you a service to-day which we cannot too highly appreciate. The graves have been alluded to, and it is well they should be; but before we go out let us remember the cradles. There are ears too young to hear our speech to-night, and eyes not yet instructed in vision, so that they may read the motto above our heads; and there is one man sitting here before you who has done a service for this class that I can not overrate. A hand has been reached into the past; into the dark past of tradition, and out of it fetched something more valuable than gold; and it is more pleasant for me to think of it, because that hand is aged, and whether it reaches backward or forward, it will reach not many years again. The man who has done you a service you can never repay is Rev. Dr. Linsley. We cannot consent to separate until this aged man, who has long been your teacher, and who has done you such service, shall have received a public expression of your respect by this audience rising in his honor."

I shall never forget the thrill that went through that great audience, as rising to their feet, Mr. Murray said: "Receive, my aged friend, this mark of a peoples' respect. The thanks of men are common, but the thanks of the multitude are few." For more than forty-six years have I carried in my memory the burning incidents of that day. No one present has lived to forget and again and again has the story been told to the new generation, those who now stand in the place of the fathers.

I cannot conclude this chapter without referring to George A. Gordon, D.D., pastor of the old South Church, Boston. He came to Greenwich, as the pastor of the Second Congregational Church, when he was on the sunny side of thirty.

He was born in Scotland. He has often told of his first job in America, when as a greenhorn he hired out to a blacksmith, who never paid him. After that he took care of the Rev. Mr. Angier's furnace in Cambridge who saw that the boy had brains and educated him. This same Mr. Angier afterwards supplied the pulpit of the Second Congregational Church to which Mr. Gordon was subsequently called.

Before these two men met Mr. Gordon had but one given name—George, but afterwards Angier was inserted as the middle name.

Mr. Angier preaching at Greenwich suggested young Gordon for the pastorate and he accepted although qualified for a larger field. To a man of his ability and resources the Greenwich church was as restricted and confining as a flying cage to a skylark.

And yet when the summons came from the old South Church he hesitated. He loved Greenwich and his people and they loved him. The town was more rural thirty years ago and he loved the country. Round Island, Field Point and all the territory near were open to his saunterings. His parishioners besought him not to leave and for two years he heeded them and refused to go.

On the 23d of October, 1912, he came back to Greenwich to take part in his old church in the installation of Rev. Charles F. Taylor. He was the same Gordon, refined and matured. He spoke feelingly of the other days but nothing he said had more pathos and love in it than his allusion to a roll of paper among his revered treasures. Tied with a blue ribbon, the paper once white, but now yellow with time, contained six hundred and fifty signatures of those who thus asked him to remain their pastor. Some were children, now active men and women and many were old men who have gone to the hereafter. And then turning to the new pastor he said: "There is the same fountain of loyalty and love here as there was thirty years ago."

There have been four Congregational churches in the village, all occupying nearly the same location. Of the first house of worship, in which the Rev. Mr. Morgan preached, little is known, except that it was 32x26 and like the one in "Old Town" (now Sound Beach).

The second was erected in 1730 and was a plain barn-like structure, 50x35, surmounted by a tower which was taken down in 1749. There was a door at each end and one in the side. Twenty square pews were located about the sides of the house and there were five in the south gallery.

This structure gave way to the third house in 1798. It was in this building that stoves were introduced in 1818, in the face of great opposition. On the first Sunday of their appearance the congregation was almost overcome by the heat, but it was learned after the service that the stoves contained no fires and that the intense heat was but the force of imagination.

When the foundation for the present building was laid, it became necessary to move the old church about one hundred feet south. Here it was continued in use till December 5, 1858, when Rev. Dr. Linsley delivered in it the last sermon, which was in the form of a commemorative discourse.

EARLY CHURCH BUILDINGS
Insert—Rev. Joel Mann

SECOND CONGREGATIONAL CHURCH

The following year the building was sold to Thomas A. Mead and Amos M. Brush, who subsequently moved it to the corner of Putnam Avenue and Sherwood Place, then Mechanic Street.

But before moving it, the steeple was cut down. The columns at the belfry were first sawed nearly off, Stephen Sillick and Henry Waring Howard, then apprentices to Stephen Sherwood, doing the work. A long rope had first been attached to the top of the spire and carried down beyond the Town House and tied to an ox cart belonging to Joseph Brush. Mr. Brush drove a sturdy pair of cattle, that he claimed were equal to pulling the moon, if he could get a line to it. Everything being made fast the cattle were started. The line grew taut; the steeple bent, then vibrated under the increased tension, while the ox cart went up in the air, and falling back to its place the steeple snapped cart and oxen more than fifty feet up the road and landed them in one promiscuous heap. The steeple was finally conquered by loading the cart with heavy stones.

This building, after its removal, has been spoken of in Chapter II. Here Dr. Sylvester Mead first appeared as the successor of Dr. Aiken in the drug business, and George E. Scofield began to learn the art of prescription filling.

On the afternoon of July 3, 1866, a small boy thoughtlessly tossed a lighted fire cracker upon the roof of the old church and at sun-set it was a smoking ruin.

OTHER DAYS IN GREENWICH

But the present church building every one knows. Of Leopold Eidlitz, an architect of fame, it has been said that of all his successful designs, none is more graceful than that beautiful spire. Where can you

ROCKEFELLER PARK IN 1860
The large elm at the left now shades the home of Charles
A. Taylor on Connecticut Avenue

drive in Greenwich and lose sight of it? You see it as you ascend every hill. The gleam of its weather vane reaches every valley. Between the delicate lines of its open columns the setting sun will often pierce till it looks as though it were a part of the azure blue, without a foundation upon earth, resting in the clouds.

CHAPTER XI

EIGHTY years ago, the road to Piping Point, was eighteen feet wide, dusty in summer and muddy in winter and yet it was a much traveled way. Did it not lead all Stanwich and Banksville to the home of the humble clam, and what Round Hill man has not traveled it in search of the hardy black fish?

How many hundred thousand bushels of potatoes have been hauled over it to find their way from Daniel Merritt's dock to the city of New York? When the crop was ready for the diggers the farmers often worked all night under a bright October moon and in the early morning their teams waited their turn to unload at the dock.

What is now Arch Street was then the only continuation of our present Greenwich Avenue.

Beyond was the farm of Daniel S. Mead, the grandfather of Oliver D. Mead and south of the present railway line, on Rocky Neck, was a forest of great trees, beneath which the underbrush grew rank and tangled.

The road to Piping Point, as the old records term it, deflected to the southwest from a point near the present Police Headquarters, No. 270 Greenwich Avenue, and ran over the top of a knoll that oc-

[117]

cupied what is now the front lawn of the Havemeyer school.

On the crest of this knoll, at least twenty feet high, stood, within my recollection, a snug little cottage. Near the front door on the south side of the house a long well sweep pointed to the north star and the water that came up in the oaken bucket was cool and sweet. How many teamsters have stopped for the cooling draught and to gossip a moment, with the little old lady who lived there! Not a house then save one from that hill to the head of the creek and no trees to shade the cultivated fields. Can you imagine the view the little house had from its vine embowered porch?

Further north on the east side of this same way was a never failing spring much thought of by those same teamsters. It bubbled up at the top of a knoll on the spot where now stands the Prescott building at 105 Greenwich Avenue, and when that building was erected in 1891 the spring was uncovered and at considerable expense turned into the sewer. It had been covered up many years before, when Dr. Lewis owned the farm and it was sorely missed. It had come to be considered common property and the foot path that led to it was worn deep by the passage of many feet. It was a cozy nook, too, for the bushes grew high above it and kept the sun from its limpid waters. To what degradation has it fallen that it should be buried beneath a brick building and emptied into a sewer!

[118]

But as early as 1854 the road had lost much of its rural aspect. The railroad, then in operation five years, had brought the town nearer to New York.

HENRY M. BENEDICT
President Gold Exchange Bank, N. Y.
Warden, Borough of Greenwich
1824–1896

Outsiders had discovered the natural beauties of the place and had begun to settle here.

Among those who came about 1850 was Henry M. Benedict, a man of great ability, of magnificent figure and large wealth. He resided on Putnam Avenue till 1873, when he removed to Brooklyn. He died in 1896 at Sunset Park, N. Y.

Mr. Benedict did not like the road to the depot and he set about to have it widened. Application was made to the selectmen but there was a general opposition to the scheme. Eighteen feet was deemed quite wide enough, because it had answered the purpose for generations. The selectmen perhaps were of the same opinion, for nothing was done. Mr. Benedict then employed Julius B. Curtis, a young lawyer of Greenwich, subsequently located until his death in Stamford. He brought an action to the County Court, then having jurisdiction, and after some time accomplished his purpose and opened the road, which then received the name of Greenwich Avenue.

With the widening of the street real estate began to look up. It was considered a side street, Putnam Avenue, then called Main Street, claiming all the pretensions of a business thoroughfare. As a residence street Greenwich Avenue was considered attractive. Any part of it commanded a fine Sound view and there was no obstruction to the refreshing southwest breeze.

Edwin Mead, a brother of Daniel S. Mead, now residing in California, at the age of ninety-three, came into possession, by inheritance, of a number of acres north of Elm Street. He had his land surveyed and divided into three-quarter-acre plots, offering them at six hundred dollars each. In those days such a plot was considered very small and the price asked quite extravagant.

William M. Tiers bought the corner lot, where afterwards, for so many years resided Dr. T. S. Pinneo. Isaac Weed bought the plot now occupied by the library and Shadrach M. Brush secured the plot still owned by his sons, S. Augustus and Henry L. Brush. Most of these sales were made in the spring and summer of 1855. I have told something of this avenue in Chapter II, and

SHADRACH M. BRUSH
1818–1903

In early days did a large business at Mianus. Subsequently conducted lumber business at Rocky Neck.

there is very little left to say concerning its progress except what is known to this generation, and that is not the province of this volume.

The old town building, now occupied by Mayer H. Cohen, is still the property of the town. Its story is told in Chapter XX.

From the head of the avenue was once a steep hill; rustic old stone walls were on portions of either side and young men and boys found it a convenient place to coast in winter, as late as thirty years ago.

Hanford Mead had a tannery where Benjamin Lockwood's restaurant is located and later, on September 4, 1854, Henry Held opened a market in a building he had erected near the tan vats. He was then the owner of all the land on the west side of the avenue from Peter Acker's to Capt. Lyon's, where the Trust Company's building is located.

A Port Chester newspaper came out with the announcement that Mr. Held was about to build "a new, elegant, imposing and commodious market building." This was an innovation that was unlooked for and besides it was the beginning of a "side street" and a street, too, that did not possess popular favor. When the newspaper later came out with a description of the building "to be filled with brick and surmounted by a balloon frame," it was the general opinion about the village that anything in the nature of a balloon, was decidedly unstable, was likely to be disastrously affected by air currents, and on a windy day would be a menace to those who happened along that way.

In Peter Acker's store the subject of the balloon frame was discussed night after night and many a hot word was passed over the subject. No one disputed the undesirableness of such a structure—it was not that: they were all opposed to the balloon frame, and they couldn't agree as to how such a thing could be framed. Solomon S. Gansey said he believed they had been used some in other parts—"in mild climates where the wind blew easy"— but they had generally been set up where they were protected by forest trees. He thought he could frame one, and he had a theory of construction which most of the others failed to favor and hence the heated argument over Held's balloon frame.

But the building went up, and as the first building in town to be framed after the balloon method, it attracted wide local attention. For those days it was really fine. Inside, the marble top counters, against the wall, meat hooks of the latest device, the pictures of fat cattle and the polished horns that stood out from the wall, with streaming red and blue ribbons at their tips, made an impressive appearance. Mr. Held was popular with all his

CAPT. W. L. LYON
1808–1858

customers. No more honest or conscientious man ever lived. He had many opportunities to invest in Wall Street and to buy Greenwich real estate, but he availed himself of Wall Street opportunities not at all and his local real estate holdings were never large.

One morning Capt. Wm. L. Lyon, who then owned the Voorhis property, tried to sell him all the land south of the market, now No. 74 Greenwich Avenue to where the Greenwich drug store stands, for eleven hundred dollars "and trade it out in meat."

It is not surprising that Mr. Held promptly declined to pay what was then a large price for land he did not require.

The old man was faithful to his market patrons for many years and at last one afternoon down at Indian Harbor, his life went out with the ebbing tide that flowed under his window, a man honored and respected by all who knew him.

CHAPTER XII

DURING the last days of President Buchanan's administration, and up to the time that Fort Sumter was fired on, politics in Greenwich were so warm that they sometimes became bitter.

The South had many sympathizers, called Copperheads, while those who favored the abolition of slavery, at whatever cost, were called Black Republicans. From this it must not be inferred that no member of the Democratic party favored the abolition of slavery, for there were many among them known as War Democrats, who agreed on that point with members of the other party, sometimes termed Radicals. The shooting of young Col. Ellsworth, the first blood shed in the war—it was really a murder—created great excitement, as it probably did all over the country. His photograph encircled with a broad band of black, was on sale at the local stores and many in the village displayed the picture on their front mantels.

Long special trains of cars often went through, the bands playing and the car platforms filled with soldiers. In some instances flags were displayed along the sides of the cars and beneath the folds of the flag appeared the name and number of the regiment and company.

ELNATHAN HUSTED
Co. I 10th C. V.
Died in service, 1864

The boys about the village found a great deal of interest in watching these trains and discussing among themselves the places from whence the soldiers hailed, all of them coming from Maine and other eastern States. Being too young to enlist, they declared that they regretted it and one or two made application for the position of drummer boy, but with what success I do not recall.

A fine, tall flag pole was erected at the foot of Lafayette Place through the efforts of William Scofield, and a few years ago, when the watering-trough was put there, the decayed remains of the old pole were taken out of the ground. The pole remained there and was in use as late as 1872, when it had so far decayed that it was removed.

ALVORD PECK
En. 1861 Co. I 10th C. V., Dis. 1864

ISAAC L. MEAD
Serg. Co. I 17th Ct. V.
1834–1913

CORP. WILLIAM BIRD
En. 1861. Dis. 1864. Co. I 10th
C. V. Br. 1842. D. 1901

WILLIAM PURDY
En. Co. I 10th C. V. 1862. Dis.
close of war

SERG. CALEB M. HOLMES
Fell in battle before Richmond
Oct. 13, 1864, aged 22, while in
command Co. I 10th C. V.

This pole, when it was first contemplated, was a subject of great delight and anticipation. For several months it lay along the side of Lafayette Place, while the carpenters and painters smoothed and polished its surface. Lying prostrate it looked very short and when it was finally raised and a topmast added, it exceeded the expectations of all. A magnificent flag, purchased by subscription, floated from the mast head every day.

JOHN BUSH MATTHEWS
Co. I 10th C. V. Served 3 yrs.

JAMES GERALD
Co. I 10th C. V.
En. 1861. Died in service

Standing where Oscar Tuthill and his brother conduct the Round Hill Farms Dairy, was a small frame two-story building, which subsequently was used by the town for public offices and in 1874 was hired by Henry B. Marshall, who therein established the beginning of the present Marshall's Market. During the early days of the war this building was used as an enlisting

[129]

station. Billy Acker with his drum and William Johnson with his fife were constantly at work drumming enthusiasm into possible recruits. It was an attractive front door for the boys who hung around while the recruiting officer measured the applicants and took their descriptions before including them in the list of raw recruits.

MAJOR D. M. MEAD
Who went out as Captain

Company I of the Tenth Conn. Volunteers was the first to go to the seat of war and included some of the finest young men in town. Daniel Merritt Mead, afterwards Major, was the captain of this company and for some weeks before they left he was about the streets in his bright new uniform; on drill days with his sword at his side.

We thought him a grand and imposing figure, as indeed he was, and he received the admiration of all the boys, without, probably, realizing it.

My brother, L. P. Hubbard, Jr., had enlisted for three years in a Manchester, New Hampshire, Regi-

LT. THOMAS R. MEAD
En. 1861. Died in service Capt.
of Co. G 10th C. V.

LT. DAVID W. MEAD
En. Co. I 10th C. V. 1862. Resigned 1863

WILLIAM
MORRISON
En. 1862

Co. I 10th C. V.
Discharged close
of war

HENRY H. MEAD
Co. I 10th C. V. Died in service
Apr. 20th, 1862, at age of 21

SILAS E. MEAD
Born 1844. En. 1861 Co. I 10th
C. V. Discharged close of war

ment and this gave me a good standing with the other boys of my own age, whose elder brothers and fathers had enlisted. Subsequently when my brother made us a visit on furlough I was very proud to walk by his side as he went about the village in his uniform.

L. P. HUBBARD, Jr.
Served 3 Years, Wounded Battle of Bull Run

Finally on a beautiful Autumn day in 1861—September 25—came the departure of Company I. The soldier boys, for they were generally about twenty-one years of age, gathered in the old Town Hall which stood where the Soldiers' monument so appropriately stands.

I quote from the diary of Capt. Daniel Merritt Mead:

"On the morning of the "25th of September we "found ourselves ready to leave, with about fifty-five "men for rendezvous.

"Our friends, at home, by thousands escorted us to "the depot, having procured a brass band from New "Rochelle. We marched to Putnam Hill to meet an "expected escort from Mianus which failed to come. "Then we returned to the Congregational Church "where prayer was offered by Rev. Dr. Linsley and

[133]

"a sword presented to the Captain. The presenta-
"tion speech was made by Julius B. Curtis in behalf
"of the donors, who were Stephen G. White, Wil-
"liam Smith, Lyman Mead, and Charles H. Seaman.

"An affectionate leave-taking from friends was
"then had, when we took up our line of March to the
"depot. On our way cheers and tears were alternat-
"ing. At the depot a speech was made by Dr.

WILLIAM SMITH
1798–1872

LYMAN MEAD
1824–1895

"James H. Hoyt and replied to by the Captain,
when leave-taking was renewed and continued until
"the arrival of the train, when we left in the last car
"for Hartford."

Many of the soldiers were members of Dr. Linsley's church and while I was too young to appreciate
his prayer, it was said to have been very fervent. I
recall how his hands trembled as he extended them
in his final benediction.

All the village boys followed the soldiers and min-

CAPT. SELLECK L. WHITE
Co. I 10th C. V.
Died in service Aug. 1864

LT. W. L. SAVAGE
Co. I 10th C. V.
En. 1861. Dis. 1864

SERG.
NORVEL GREEN
En. 1861

Co. I 10th C. V.
Re-enlisted
1864

CORP. ALEXANDER FERRIS
Color bearer Co. I 10th C. V.
Killed at Drury's Bluff, 1864

CORP. WILLIS H. WILCOX
En. 1861. Served 3 yrs. Co. I 10th
C. V.

gled in the crowd that filled the walk on either side of the dusty road.

Until five years ago a black mulberry tree grew on the east side of Greenwich Avenue just below the row of new brick stores. As I reached the mulberry tree there was a slight pause in the ranks. Lieutenant Benjamin Wright and Sergeant William Long, marching side by side,

JAMES H. HOYT, M.D.
1829–1875
Surgeon General State of Connecticut

drew near. I noticed the dust across the shoulders of their new uniforms, and then came to me the

CHARLES H. SEAMAN
1819–1899

impression that one of them would never come back. And so it was— Long was one of the first to lay down his life.

Company I was remarkable in the fact that its ranks included no less than twelve pair of brothers. They were Erastus and James Burns, David and Jared Finch; John and Holly Hubbard; William and Drake Marshall; Charles and John McCann;

[137]

William and George Jerman; Stephen and Henry Brady; George and William Robbins; Louis and John Schaffer; Henry and Warren Scott; Aaron and John Sherwood, and John and Thomas Wilson.

LIEUT. BENJAMIN WRIGHT

In addition to this there were three instances where father and son stood side by side, and in the ranks of the Company were three brothers-in-law.

After the soldiers had departed they were constantly in mind and after every engagement the papers were carefully scanned for news of boys at the front. Letters came often, the envelopes covered with spirited pictures of war scenes. Indeed, plain white envelopes were seldom seen in those days, a flag in colors usually occupying the left hand corner.

The Sanitary Commission had a branch here, made up of ladies who sewed for the well soldiers and put up bandages and lint for the sick and wounded.

Boxes were sent out by the families of soldiers filled with such simple things as corn meal, onions, salt and pepper; essential, but often difficult to get at the front.

Quite frequently the great flag hung at half mast and then the boys would wonder who had gone and whether by shot, shell or disease.

There were military funerals of which I recall that of William Donohue and later the more imposing funerals of Sergeant William Long, Thomas R. Mead, Henry Mead, and Caleb M. Holmes, all of Company I, also that of Oliver D. Benson of another regiment.

COL. OTIS

Of the 10th Reg. Conn. Volunteers. Not a Greenwich man but beloved by every member of Co. I

When Major Daniel Merritt Mead was brought home in a dying condition the sympathy of all was aroused, and as he lay sick for two weeks in the old homestead on the Post Road many a prayer was offered for his recovery. But he passed away on the

19th day of September, 1862, at the early age of twenty-eight.

SERG. WILLIAM LONG
En. 1861 Co. I 10th C. V. Died
Morris Island, 1863

His funeral was held in the Second Congregational Church and I recall that his military hat and sword rested upon the coffin. The church was crowded to such an extent that the support under the west gallery snapped like the report of a pistol with the weight of the people. Few realized the cause of the peculiar noise.

It was a sad morning in April, 1865, when the news of the assassination of President Lincoln reached Greenwich. Members of both political parties bowed their heads in sorrow and the emblems of mourning were universal.

The following chapter contains an account of the sermon preached by Rev. William H. H. Murray on this occasion.

AMOS MEAD LYON
Master's Mate U. S. N., 1861–1865.
Last year on staff of Admr.
Porter. In several important
engagements including Fort
Fisher

CHAPTER XIII

REV. WILLIAM HENRY HARRISON
MURRAY was born in Guilford, Conn.,
April 26, 1840. He was graduated from Yale and
from a school of Theology, becoming acting pastor
of the Second Congregational Church at the age of
twenty-four. He remained as long as the church
could keep him, but in 1866 the First Congregational
Church of Meriden offered him a liberal salary and
he left.

When he came to Greenwich he was, in years,
scarcely more than a boy, yet he had the poise and
dignity of a mature man. He stood over six feet
in height, was straight as an arrow, and of massive
physique. His large, well-shaped head was covered
with abundant black hair. His eyes fairly glittered
with life and animation.

He had an unbroken colt that he kept at Col.
Thomas A. Mead's, also a row boat on the Sound.
In almost every Congregational home were displayed, in conspicuous places, the photographs of
Mr. and Mrs. Murray. All of the old generation
remember him distinctly. The younger generation
has little knowledge of him, because he disappeared

[141]

from public life many years ago and the old photographs have been hidden away or destroyed. He was clever, handsome and magnetic and fearless in

W. H. H. MURRAY
At the age of 24

his preaching. His originality was unique, usually pleasing and often startling.

In speaking of himself in the latter years of his life he once said: "I was born of poor parents, as the majority of New England boys were in my day. There had never been a rich rascal in our family, nor did I come of literary stock. No college-bred dunce had ever handicapped us with his incapable respectability. I had, therefore, a fair start. The Connecticut Murrays were not afraid to tell the truth to any man and could swear heartily at hypocritical meanness—at least my father could. At the age of seven I began to earn my own living, as every boy should. At fourteen I read all the books I could lay my hands on. At sixteen I began to prepare for college. I had no help, no encouragement. My father opposed me in my efforts and my mother said nothing. My old neighbors in their ignorance said: 'I wonder what Bill Murray thinks he can make of himself?' But I persevered. I was sensitive to ridicule. I had an impediment in my speech, but I had taken hold of the rope of knowledge with a good grip and I held on.

"I started for Yale with four dollars and sixty-eight cents in my pocket and two small carpet bags in my hands—one for my few books, the other for my few clothes. While at the university I was urged by family and friends, more than once, to give it up. One winter I lived for four weeks on a diet that cost fifty-six cents a week: Indian meal and water—not over much meal and a good deal too much water. I went through the entire course—I don't remember that I lost a week. I was graduated crammed full of the knowledge of books from enormous reading, seasoned with a fair proficiency in the studies of the curriculum, but not over seasoned. Then without pause I went to East Windsor, where they take young men as Christians and make them over into Calvinists, and studied old world theology."

While at Greenwich Mr. Murray made his first excursion into the Adirondack wilderness. It was then almost an unknown territory. While at Meriden he passed his summer vacations in the Adirondacks and wrote to the *Meriden Recorder* a series of letters that were afterwards incorporated into a book entitled "Adventures in the Wilderness," which made him a literary celebrity and gave him a name that always stuck—"Adirondack Murray."

About the same time appeared in the *Atlantic Monthly* a story entitled "A Ride with a Mad Horse in a Freight Car," which was said to contain the best description of a horse in action that was ever written.

Before coming to Greenwich, Mr. Murray had married the daughter of Sheldon Hull, a prosperous farmer of Essex, Conn. Her sister, Ida Hull, lived with them while in Greenwich and attended the Academy.

The news of the assassination of President Lincoln reached Greenwich on Saturday morning at eight o'clock. Before noon a meeting of the pastor and deacons of the Second Congregational Church was held and it was voted to drape the interior of the church in black. Mr. Murray agreed to preach an appropriate sermon the following morning.

A number of the active young men and women, assisted by Mr. Murray, had completed the decorations by sunset. They covered the front of the galleries, twisted the black muslin about the posts, looped it around the pulpit and strung it above the organ, till the great edifice looked heavy with the folds of black, from which were visible, here and there, the bright colors of the stars and stripes.

After it was all finished, Murray said: "I'll take a little outdoor exercise after supper and when I return I'll prepare the special sermon for to-morrow."

Late that night there was a light in his study in the church. He had a window open and he could hear the voices of the peepers in the distance. His heavy black hair hung like a great shock over his brow. His thoughts, at times, came too fast for his fingers; but at the weird hour when the night begins to change to another day, he laid down his pen, put out the light, and with body erect as in the morning, he strode across the yard to the parsonage door.

The next morning as he arose to deliver his sermon to an immense audience, his face for a moment clouded with sorrow. His voice, always heavy, resonant and musical, was at first husky, but as he caught the sympathy of his hearers, his voice cleared and, without a note, he delivered one of the most eloquent discourses ever heard in that church.

He began: "To-day the wicked triumph and the "good are brought low. Two days ago the Republic "stood erect, strong and valiant; her foot advanced "and countenance radiant with hope. To-day she "lies prostrate upon the ground, her features stained

[145]

"with the traces of recent grief, and her voice lifted
"in lamentation."

The sermon of this boy of twenty-four was filled
with the wisdom of a sage. As he drew toward the
close he said: "Nor is he wholly gone! He lives;
"not in bodily presence, but yet he lives, in the his-
"tory of his times, in the memory of his age—in the
"affections of us all. His name will not be forgot-
"ten. The living of to-day will tell it to the unborn
"and they, in turn, will repeat it to the remotest age.
"Amid the doings of the great of every clime will his
"deeds be recorded. Among the teachings of the
"wise will his sayings be written. In galleries where
"wealth gathers the faces of the loved and the re-
"nowned will his portrait be suspended, and in hum-
"bler homes and in lowlier hearts will his face and
"his memory be retained, until the present has be-
"come the past, and the children cease to be moved
"by the traditions of the fathers.

"We cannot measure him to-day. Years must
"pass before his influence on his age can be estimated.
"It needs the contrast of history to reveal his great-
"ness. In the native vigor of his intellect, in the sin-
"cerity of his purpose, in the originality of his views,
"in the simplicity of his faith, and in his sympathy
"for the oppressed, what potentate of his time will
"bear a comparison with this backwoodsman of
"America? Untaught in the formalities of courts,
"he aped not their customs. Unostentatious, he as-
"pired to nothing beyond his reach and seemed to

[146]

"reach more than he aspired after. He was incapa-
"ble of bitterness, and in this doth his greatness most
"appear, that having defamers, he heeded them not,
"persecuted by enemies he hated them not, reviled by
"inferiors, he retorted not."

It is sad to think that a man as capable as Murray
should have gone to pieces, like a ship on a ledge.
Leaving Meriden, he was the settled pastor of Park
Street Church, Boston, at the age of twenty-eight.
But in Boston his career seemed a striking case of a
square peg trying to fit into a round hole. Sport of
all kinds fascinated the man, and the conventionali-
ties that hedge about the ministerial cloth became exceedingly distasteful to him.

To the Park Street Church deacons it was equally
distasteful to have the name of their pastor connected
constantly with horse racing. Whether Mr. Murray
ever risked money on the races, was never established,
but that he organized the Boston Buckboard Co. to
introduce a trotting sulky, deemed by him of superior
quality and put a good deal of time into the business
of breeding Morgan horses at his Guilford farm,
there is no question. At one time the Guilford estate, which included the old homestead, which he had
purchased after it went out of the family, was worth
seventy-two thousand dollars, a fact quite sufficient
to reassure those whom Mr. Murray had persuaded
to invest heavily in the Buckboard Co.

Racing and religion soon began to be blended by
Mr. Murray in a manner most severely criticized.

He owned and edited a weekly paper called *The Golden Rule,* which had a large number of subscribers in Greenwich. In this paper matters pertaining to the turf and the church were treated with so loose an attempt at impartiality that there seemed at times to be a leaning towards favoring the turf the

THOMAS RITCH
In 1880

more. As a natural consequence, in 1874, he was forced to resign from Park Street Church. But for the following three years he drew great audiences to Music Hall where he preached liberty, free speech and independent action.

As a pulpit orator he was incomparable. There was a peculiar charm in his delivery, a magnetism in his presence and a profound logic in his reasoning, which rendered his talks positive rhetorical studies. His religion, at this time, was the doctrine of common sense.

There was no egotism in his manner, no narrowness in his ideas. To hear him was to realize his powers of mind. To meet him was to comprehend his graces of manner, and to know him was to appreciate his goodness of heart.

However he certainly had no business ability. *The Golden Rule* failed and to the buckboard enterprise there came a financial crisis. One morning the pastor, author, editor and manufacturer was missing. From Texas he sent a letter to the Boston newspapers declaring that business had called him to that distant

MRS. W. H. H. MURRAY
In 1864

State. He insisted that he had always intended to retire from public life when he was forty and that it was in fulfillment of this determination that he left Boston a few weeks before his fortieth birthday.

In the fall of 1881 Murray conceived a project of shipping Texas wood to Chicago and other northern manufacturing centers, but as the scheme necessitated the transportation of material which could be secured better and cheaper nearer home, its chance of success was slight. Yet Murray so believed in it that he built a mill on the Guadalupe, about forty miles from San Antonio, and went there to conduct it. He also induced people to invest in this singular enterprise. At this time he became, himself, a teamster. He dressed in brown overalls, cowhide boots and a blue and white checked shirt. Then as he left New England—with many debts behind him; so Mr. Murray left Texas.

In the winter of 1883, the late Thomas Ritch told me that he found him running a restaurant called the "Snow Shoe" in Montreal where Murray himself, in cap and apron, had cooked and served for him a plate of buckwheat cakes. Here he met so many of his old parishioners that the restaurant actually served as an entering wedge for the man's return to the world again.

The winter of 1884 he was back again on the Boston lecture platform. That same winter, or the next, he lectured in Ray's Hall in Greenwich. A few of his old friends were present, but nearly every one had forgotten the eloquent preacher of twenty years before. And yet, after all his vicissitudes, his charm of old had not departed. That night he read from his own works "How John Norton, the trapper, kept his Christmas," a vivid and exquisitely pathetic description of a lonely mountaineer's perilous tramp to insure a happy Christmas to another. As the story was read, with the same deep resonant voice of old, those who heard it could not but do homage to the humanity and genius of its writer.

Before I close this painful chapter I must recur to Mrs. Murray or the story will be incomplete. She was a remarkable woman, possessed of unusual intellectual power. The year that her husband left her she entered the New York Medical School for a term. Then she went to Europe and for three years studied in Vienna Medical College and finally was graduated in surgery as well as medicine, with high honors. She was the first American woman to receive, in Europe, a diploma entitling her to practice as a surgeon. Returning to her native land she opened an office in New Haven.

The same year that his wife divorced him Mr. Murray married Miss Frances M. Rivers of Montreal, a Catholic. With her and their four daughters he long lived happily in retirement at the old homestead in Guilford and there he died in 1906 in the same room in which he was born. His body was laid at rest under an old apple tree near the house.

The following lines were written by Mr. Murray in 1867 as a prelude to a sermon on Faithfulness:

> The play is done—the curtain drops
> Slow falling to the prompter's bell;
> A moment yet the actor stops,
> And looks around to say farewell,
> It is an irksome word and task,
> And when he's laughed and said his say,

[151]

OTHER DAYS IN GREENWICH

He shows, as he removes the mask,
A face that's anything but gay.
So each shall mourn, in life's advance,
Dear hopes, dear friends, untimely killed—
Shall grieve for many a forfeit chance,
And longing passion unfulfilled.
Amen! Whatever fate be sent,
Pray God the heart may kindly glow,
Although the head with cares be bent,
And whitened with the winter's snow.

CHAPTER XIV

A T the opening of the nineteenth century there were but three prominent trees on the main country road from Putnam Hill to Toll Gate Hill. The husbandman's ax kept the hedge rows trimmed and ornamental trees were rarely set out, as they shaded the growing crops.

The three trees that held their branches high in the air were plainly visible from vessels cruising in the Sound. They were button-ball trees; one stood in front of the old Hobby tavern on what is now the J. H. Fennessy property on East Putnam Avenue; another spread its immense limbs over Dearfields, the home of Richard Mead, later of Col. Thomas A. Mead; and the other, until 1911, stood in front of the Peter Acker homestead on Putnam Avenue. This latter tree was the smallest of the trio, but had been sturdy and vigorous at the opening of the Revolutionary War.

The Hobby tavern stood almost exactly on the ground occupied by Mr. Fennessy's beautiful house of antique style. Capt. John Hobby had been active in the eighteenth century, but on the 13th of May, 1802, when probably an old man, he sold all his Horse

[153]

Neck real estate to Hannah Courtney. This consisted of twenty-two acres, near the Meeting House, on both sides of the Post Road. He bounded the southerly tract on the east by land of Jared Mead and on the south by land of the Rev. Dr. Isaac Lewis.

RESIDENCE OF BEALE N. LEWIS

Erected 1807. Subsequently the home of Henry M. Benedict and Dr. William Guy Peck

Subsequent deeds bound it on the west by land of Dr. Lewis, and it apparently extended east to what is now the Frederick Mead place, west to the present line of Mason Street and south to land now owned by the Greenwich Hospital. The tract on the north side of the road included property now known as the Elms and a considerable tract west of it. But the land still further west, belonging to Dr. Carl E. Martin and Walter M. Anderson and Ada M. Cook, belonged to Thomas Hobby, probably a brother of the Captain.

It is clear that Captain Hobby lived on the south side of the road and probably on the commanding eminence where Henry M. Benedict lived so many years, and afterward owned and occupied by Professor Wm. Guy Peck of West Point and Columbia College. That the house had long been an inn, and that it was of ample dimensions, shaded by the great button-ball tree, there is no doubt. But the shrewd Captain Hobby in his deed to Miss Courtney, a New York lady of wealth and social position, makes no allusion to a tavern, inn, or public house, but described the buildings as a "mansion house and barn."

Miss Courtney paid $2,843.75 for the handsomest piece of property in the village of Horse Neck. At that time, however, it could hardly be termed a village. There were but few houses, well scattered and whatever commercial interests Greenwich had were centered at Mianus, where the Town Clerk's office was located.

From the hilltop purchased by Miss Courtney was an unobstructed view in all directions. It was said that travelers by stage coach along the Post Road anticipated with pleasure that part of the trip from Putnam Hill to Toll Gate Hill where the view of the Sound was unbroken and unobstructed the entire distance.

My father made the stage coach trip from New

York to Boston in 1833, and stopped at what was then the Mansion House, since called the Lenox House, kept by Augustus Lyon. He (my father) often referred to the fact that the two front rooms of the present Lenox House, are identical with the two front rooms of that ancient hostelry—the Mansion House.

Hannah Courtney owned the Hobby property but

DR. WM. G. PECK
1820–1892

five years. It is easy to imagine that she did not find it uninteresting, but that it was remote from New York, and that the means of transportation by sloop or stage coach were not agreeable. At all events on November 11, 1807, for the consideration of $500, she sold it to Beale N. Lewis. It is not likely that Miss Courtney suffered such a loss, or that Mr. Lewis made such a good bargain as to actually get the property for $500, which was doubtless a nominal consideration. They were cousins.

Beale N. Lewis was also from New York City, and was a son of the Rev. Dr. Isaac Lewis. He was an able lawyer of large wealth. As soon as he acquired the land, he removed the Hobby tavern and built what was then considered a grand mansion. It was not deep but it was wide, built like three cubes, a

[156]

large one in the center, and one at each end for wings. He died possessed of the property in the spring of 1817, leaving a widow, Elizabeth Lewis, but no lineal heirs. His death occurred seven years before that of his distinguished father.

On May 11, 1829, the brothers and sisters of Beale N. Lewis conveyed the same twenty-two acres to Peter Tillott, James Tillott and Susan Seymour. They were probably speculators as they subsequently owned other land in town, and did considerable conveyancing. But the venture does not appear to have been profitable as they held the land till April 4, 1833, when they sold it at cost to Alvan Mead.

In 1833 Cornelia J. Graham and Mary E. Graham, sisters, were conducting a school on the north side of the Post Road where they owned considerable real estate. The Alvan Mead purchase was bounded on the east by their property. The school was carried on in the house now known as the Elms. The Tillotts and Miss Seymour must have been exceedingly tired of carrying the property as they accepted the entire purchase price in a note secured by mortgage.

Alvan Mead held it four years when, on February 6, 1837, he sold it to Obadiah Peck at a profit of $3,500.

Mr. Peck was one of our earliest real estate speculators. At that time two acres was considered a small plot. Mr. Peck was also a house builder. His aim was to improve the land with buildings and sell at a profit. He occupied the Beale N. Lewis homestead whose south windows and broad veranda commanded a splendid view of Lond Island Sound and the intervening country. Here Henry M. Benedict subsequently resided for nearly twenty years. This same house was torn down by L. V. Harkness after he purchased it from the William G. Peck estate, June 15, 1891.

But to return to Obadiah Peck. In 1854 he built the home so long occupied by the late L. P. Hubbard and now owned by Dr. Edward O. Parker. Then he built the Banks homestead recently moved by Mrs. Nathaniel Witherell to make room for the new Young Men's Christian Association building. This last venture of Mr. Peck's was disastrous and he made a bad financial failure.

Before closing this chapter and leaving the neighborhood I have been describing, I must allude to the homestead of Jared Mead, which stood where now stands the Frederick Mead homestead.

Jared Mead was the father of Alvan Mead and here Alvan was born in 1795. The house was an old-fashioned sweep-back, covered with shingles to the sills, which were close to the ground. In the center of the house was a great stone chimney which afforded an open fire place in each room of its two stories. Down the hill a short distance were the somber farm barns. Mr. Mead was a sprightly little man with a numerous family. He was prominent and active in the affairs of the Meeting House, hard by on the hill. Perhaps it should be called the Second Congregational Church but he always called it "The Meeting House."

The house was double, the hall in the center extending from the front door to the great chimney, where winding stairs with white painted banisters and a cherry rail led to the second story. On one side of this hall was the living room and the other the "best room," in later years called the "parlor." Both these rooms had grand old fire places with crane and pot hooks, blackened by the smoke and flame. The hearth was an enormous slab of blue stone, cracked across from the heat of the great logs, seven feet long, that blazed merrily all the winter day and smouldered under a bed of ashes all night.

It was Mr. Mead's duty as an active member of the church to supply the Sabbath attendants with material for their foot stoves. On Saturday an unusual supply of fire wood was stacked against the chimney jambs and by ten o'clock, Sunday, a large quantity of live coals was heaped in the spacious chimney place. As the old bell in the Meeting House was calling the parishioners to worship, they would repair to Mr. Mead's and fill their foot stoves with live coals.

It was, however, a rule of the family that no communication whatever should be had with those who called and no member of the family should go into the "best room," lest it be said that they were entertaining visitors on the Sabbath day. Those who came understood and approved of the rule. They opened the door unbidden and filling their stoves with coals went out with quiet dignity. There was no levity; no common-place remarks, only the most formal salutations were made. If anything was said, it referred to the discourse which they expected to hear, or at noon, when the stoves were replenished, concerning the sermon which they had heard. The afternoon was a repetition of the morning and the winter twilight was scarcely an hour away when the church was closed.

CHAPTER XV

A T the present time there are many people residing in Greenwich who have never heard of Boss
Tweed. Since his day the new generation has been
taught history but local characters like Tweed have
usually been ignored. During the past five years I
have made a test and have been surprised how the
once notorious politician has been forgotten. For
that reason this chapter will be devoted to the man,
without any allusion to his residence in Greenwich.

I attended Tweed's trial during the fall of 1873
and also did some clerical work for the Committee
of Seventy, being then a law student in New York
City. But much that follows in this chapter has been
culled from R. R. Wilson, who wrote a pamphlet on
the subject which is said to have been suppressed.

Until the year 1834 the Mayor of the City of New
York was chosen either by the State Council of Ap-
pointments or by the Common Council of the city.
After 1834, however, that official was elected by the
citizens. In 1846 the judiciary was made elective
and thereafter most local offices were chosen by popular vote. During the first seventy years of New
York's history as a free city the Democratic party

was the one usually in power. The Federalists and after them the Whigs occasionally secured control of affairs, but the Democrats always recovered their hold on the reins.

And without exception all the Democratic Mayors of that period owed their election to Tammany Hall, a secret association whose social and benevolent aims had been early put aside for political ones.

Business men, then as now, shrank from political activity, while the men who directed Tammany Hall knew how to drill and control the mass of poor and ignorant voters, mainly of foreign birth, who after 1840 constituted a majority of the voters. Still the majority which assured the continuance in or return to power of Tammany Hall and its allies was often a narrow one and victories were gained by fraud, intimidation and violence at the polls.

The master spirit of the organization in the early '50's was Fernando Wood, an able and resolute man, who held to the belief that success was the criterion in politics, and that almost anything was justifiable to win it.

In 1854 Wood became Mayor, and was reëlected at the end of two years. Then he quarreled with his associates in Tammany Hall and failed of a reëlection in 1858. Following this he formed Mozart Hall as a rival organization, and with its help and that of the mob in the lower wards succeeded in 1860 in defeating Tammany Hall and putting himself at the head of the City Government.

WILLIAM M. TWEED
Photo by Brady in 1871
1823–1878

THE DAYS OF BOSS TWEED

In 1862 Tammany again secured control, and for several years political corruption was rife in the City of New York.

This era of corruption was made easy by radical changes in methods of municipal administration effected in 1857. In that year a new charter was passed for the city, which, besides dividing the responsibility among the local officers, created a number of Boards and Commissions, the heads of which were not appointed by the Mayor, but elected by the voters of the city, as were also the Comptroller and Corporation Counsel.

More important still, coincident with the enactment of the new charter, a law was passed establishing for the County of New York a Board of Supervisors, chosen by popular vote, which was made independent of the city authorities, and vested with power to levy the local taxes and to direct those branches of administration which in the State at large were relegated to the county authorities.

One of the first to discover the chance for private gain at public expense made possible by the legislative changes of 1857 was William M. Tweed, a native of the city. He was a man of Scotch parentage, who after failing in business as a chairmaker had in the late '40's turned to politics as a means of livelihood.

He became first a member and then foreman of one of the volunteer fire companies of the period, known as the Big Six, thereby achieving popularity, which brought him to the attention of Tammany leaders. He was elected an Alderman of the city in 1850 and in 1853 was chosen a member of Congress. But he never cared for Washington and in 1857 he was elected Public School Commissioner and subsequently State Senator.

Meanwhile Tweed had himself elected to the newly created Board of Supervisors, of which he was four times chosen president and of which he remained the directing spirit until 1870 when it passed out of existence.

Leadership of this board, which had the power of auditing accounts, gave him an opportunity to secure various privileges which were frauds upon the city, and he made the most of it. Thus obtaining control of an obscure newspaper, he secured the passage of a bill by the legislature making it the official organ of the City Government and it was paid over a million dollars for printing the proceedings of the Common Council, which no one read.

He also established a company for the printing of blank forms and vouchers for which in one year $2,800,000 was charged. A stationers company controlled by Tweed which furnished all the stationery used in the public institutions and departments received some three million dollars a year. Tweed employed certain persons as executive heads of these companies who were also upon the city pay rolls, some receiving money for work never done. While serving as State Senator and president of the Board of Supervisors, Tweed also held the office of Deputy

[166]

Street Commissioner with "authority to appoint as many as a thousand office holders, many of whom did no work except to serve him, yet were paid out of the city treasury."

By such methods as these Tweed advanced in a few years from poverty to great wealth, and at the same time, made himself undisputed master of Tammany Hall.

In 1863 he was chosen chairman of the General Committee of the organization and Grand Sachem of the Tammany Society. In 1863, also, he assured Tammany Hall's absolute control of the city by effecting a truce with its rival organization, Wood's Mozart Hall, the price of peace being Wood's election to Congress. This truce brought Tweed two efficient lieutenants, A. Oakey Hall and Albert Cardoza, an able lawyer, who was made a judge of one of the city courts. Two other men placed upon the bench about the same time because "they could be relied upon," were John H. McCunn and George G. Barnard. Other politicians who came into close alliance with Tweed were Richard B. Connolly and Peter B. Sweeny.

In 1865 Tweed and his associates secured the election of John T. Hoffman as Mayor and three years later he was elected Governor. At that time the charge was freely made that Hoffman's election was secured by the practice of frauds described as colossal and "embracing every known method of corruption in the ballot box." Tammany Hall at the same time secured control of the legislature of the State and the Common Council of the City.

Hall succeeded Hoffman as Mayor; Connolly became City Comptroller; James Sweeny was City Chamberlain and with Tweed supreme in the street department and the Board of Supervisors, the ring which had long been in the process of formation "became completely organized and matured." Then Tweed and his lieutenants set to work to secure a new city charter, which would make doubly sure their control of the finances of the city.

This charter became a law in 1870. It abolished the Board of Supervisors, again vesting its functions in the Mayor, Recorder and Aldermen of the city, and centered responsibility for the administration of municipal affairs in the Mayor, who was given authority to appoint all his important subordinates. It surrendered the Police Department to men controlled by the ring; it re-organized the Park Department in such manner that three of the five commissioners became for five years each, tools of Tweed; it vacated the office of Street Commissioner, vesting all the powers of the office in a Commissioner of Public Works to be appointed by the Mayor for a term of four years. Tweed received the appointment. The Governor had no power to remove him on charges. He could only be impeached through charges made by the Mayor, and could only be tried in case every one of the six judges of the Court of Common Pleas was present.

THE DAYS OF BOSS TWEED

The new charter also created a Board of Apportionment made up of the Mayor, Comptroller, Commissioner of Public Works and President of the Park Department, and vested with power to make all necessary appropriations for the conduct of the city government. The men who composed this board were Hall, Connolly, Tweed and Sweeny, who had resigned the office of City Chamberlain to become President of the Park Department. And in this way the ring secured unchecked control of the expenditures of the city.

Yet another tool for plunder was forged at this time. By a special act of the legislature a Board of Audit was created and it was vested with power to examine and allow all claims against the city prior to 1870. Its purpose was to put money into the pockets of members of the ring and to reimburse them for the large sums they had been compelled to spend to secure the adoption of the new charter by the legislature. This purpose was promptly put into execution and in less than four months after its creation orders were made by the Board of Audit for the payment of claims to the amount of $6,312,500, ninety per cent. of which went into the pockets of the members of the ring.

Various other special legislative acts were passed whereby the ring had power to raise and expend nearly fifty millions of dollars in a single year.

Other laws were passed which placed the ring in more complete control of the Board of Education and of the Police and Health Boards, while there was also created a Board of Street Opening and Improvement, composed of the Mayor, Comptroller, Commissioner of Public Works and Tax Commissioner, vested with power whenever its members "deemed it for the public interest so to do" to close, open, widen or straighten any or all of the streets of the city.

The passage of these laws marked the culmination of the ring's power, and it has been said that during the winter they were being enacted "Tweed lived in Albany with all the state of a sovereign who had prodigious favors to bestow or awful penalties to enforce." There seemed never to have entered his mind a suspicion of the power of an aroused public opinion.

The story of the downfall of the ring, however, should be prefaced by a brief description of the methods which it employed to fill the pockets of its members. The opening or widening of streets was one of the most fruitful sources of illicit gain. A favorite method of fraud practiced by the ring consisted in the payment of enormously increased bills to mechanics, architects, furniture makers, and, in some instances to unknown persons for supplies and services. It was the expectation that an honest bill would be raised from sixty to ninety per cent. The average increase was such as to make it possible to give sixty-seven per cent. to the ring, the confederates being allowed to keep the thirty-three per cent., and of that thirty-three per cent. probably one-half was a fraudulent increase.

This game reached a climax in the County Court House, still standing in City Hall Park. Work on this structure was begun under a stipulation that the cost should not exceed $250,000, but before 1871 more than eight millions had been spent on it, one million of which was ultimately traced to Tweed's pocket.

When a contractor submitted a bill he would be told to swell the amount of the total, at the same time being given to understand that payment depended upon compliance with this order. Then a warrant would be drawn for the padded claim and the contractor paid a sum slightly in excess of his original bill, while the balance would be divided among the members of the ring. Nor was there any immediate danger of detection. Tweed as Commissioner of Public Works would order work done; as President of the Board of Supervisors he would see to it that the bills were passed, and then the County Auditor, who was his pliant tool, would issue warrants of payment.

All this time suspicion was rife in the community. Thomas Nast, the cartoonist for *Harper's Weekly,* was constantly illustrating the iniquities of the ring. Tweed's face and figure, with the blazing diamond in his shirt front, were always before the public. He once said, "I don't care what the papers print so much but I don't like those pictures," and in the end they were the cause of Tweed's apprehension.

[171]

OTHER DAYS IN GREENWICH

One of the politicians of the period was James O'Brien, a former sheriff of the county, who in 1871 was the leader of the Young Democracy, an organization which had for its purpose the overthrow of the power of Tweed in Tammany Hall.

Through O'Brien's influence a friend of his named Copeland had secured a place as an accountant in the office of the Comptroller. The magnitude of the city expenditures recorded in the books and the fact that these enormous payments were made to a few persons aroused Copeland's suspicions. He transcribed the figures and showed the transcript to Mr. O'Brien. They were taken by the latter to the office of a daily newspaper in the city and offered for publication but were "declined with thanks."

Thereupon Mr. O'Brien called upon George Jones, publisher of the *Times,* and handed him the transcripts from the Comptroller's accounts. Mr. Jones consulted his editorial staff and it was decided that the figures should be published. This decision was made known to Mr. O'Brien, who took the incriminating accounts, retained them for a short time and then returned them to Mr. Jones with the unconditional permission to publish.

Tweed in some manner discovered that his guilty secrets were about to be published and his desperate efforts to forestall the publication were as characteristic of him as their complete defeat was characteristic of Mr. Jones.

Tweed sent an offer to buy the *Times* at any price.

The emissary who was sent promptly reported the failure of his mission. Tweed's next move was so extraordinary that Mr. Jones' own account of what happened, taken from *Harper's Weekly* of February 22, 1890, deserves to be reproduced here.

"This conversation (between Tweed's emissary "and Mr. Jones) occurred in Jones' office in the "*Times* Building, then down town in Printing House "Square. A lawyer who was a tenant in the build-"ing sent for Mr. Jones to come to his office, as he "wished to see him on an important matter. Think-"ing that the business pertained to the building, Mr. "Jones went to the lawyer's office, and, being ushered "into a private room, was confronted by Richard "B. Connolly, the Comptroller, Tweed's partner in "crime. 'I don't want to see this man,' said Mr. "Jones and he turned to go out of the room. 'For "God's sake!' exclaimed Connolly, 'let me say one "word to you.' At this appeal Mr. Jones stopped. "Connolly then made a proposition to forego the "publication of the documents Jones had in his pos-"session, and offered him an enormous sum of money "to do this. The amount of this offer was five mil-"lion dollars. As Connolly waited for the answer "Mr. Jones said, 'I don't think the Devil will ever "make a higher bid for me than that!' Connolly "then began to plead, and drew a graphic picture with "what one could do with such a sum. He concluded "by saying: 'Why, with five million dollars you "can go to Europe and live like a prince!' 'Yes,' "said Mr. Jones, 'but I should know that I was a rascal.'"

The first installment of the accounts was printed in the *Times* July 22, 1871. They showed the payment of the sum of $5,663,646 during the years 1869 and 1870 for "repairs and furniture" for the new Court House. Each warrant was signed by Comptroller Connolly and Mayor Hall, and all were endorsed to "Ingersoll & Co.," that is, James H. Ingersoll, the agent of the ring.

The *Times* followed with other installments of secret accounts more fully revealing the extent of the plundering.

It had unmasked the ring and it pursued its advantage with extraordinary energy. An immense number of copies of each issue of the paper containing the figures, running into hundreds of thousands, was published. These proofs awakened the slumbering city. The Committee of Seventy, made up of prominent citizens, was formed early in September to obtain legal proof of the frauds revealed by the *Times* and to prosecute the offenders. At the same time Samuel J. Tilden, aided by Charles O'Conor and Francis Kernan, all three lawyers of great ability, set to work to achieve the same end. Mr. O'Conor, who was then the unchallenged leader of the New York bar, consented to aid in the investigation only upon condition that he should serve without compensation.

The task of bringing the offenders to justice appeared at the outset a difficult and nearly hopeless one. Tweed was insolent and defiant. The Board of Aldermen and all the local officers were members of the ring.

But in September, 1871, an effective weapon was unexpectedly placed in the hands of Mr. Tilden. One morning in that month he was visited by a messenger from Comptroller Connolly, who was convinced that it was Tweed's intention to offer him up as a sacrifice to appease public sentiment on the charge that the frauds had been committed in his department, by his connivance and for his exclusive benefit.

This the messenger explained to Mr. Tilden, and asked the latter's advice, suggesting that it might be best for Connolly to resign his office. Subsequently Mr. Tilden suggested that Connolly appoint Andrew H. Green, an eminent and honored lawyer, his deputy and then surrender the office to him. This was done and Mr. Green became head of the Comptroller's office, with power to examine and publish all expenditures under the ring, and to prevent any continuation of the fraudulent practices.

Though a partially successful attempt was made to burn all the vouchers soon after Mr. Green took possession, of the charred scraps remaining (great bundles of them), Mr. Tilden was engaged for some ten days in making a searching analysis, which furnished legal proof of the crime. He succeeded also in tracing through one of the banks the checks which had been issued in payment of the accounts which the vouchers purported to represent.

Indeed, Mr. Tilden's study of the vouchers and the bank accounts has often been pronounced one of the most remarkable pieces of analysis ever offered to the courts. Judge Noah Davis, of the Supreme Court, who sat upon the trial of Tweed, and heard this demonstration offered in evidence, afterwards declared it as perfect a specimen of logic and mathematical proof as the books anywhere contained.

With checks, stubs, charred vouchers and other documents, Mr. Tilden was able to show the exact amount of money stolen in each given instance and the exact division of the spoils. It was, however, then or later impossible to make an accurate estimate of the total amount of money stolen by the ring. Between 1860 and 1871 the debt of the city increased from $20,000,000 to $101,000,000, and it is believed that at least $14,000,000 of this increase represented fraud and theft.

The appointment of Mr. Green acting Comptroller thoroughly alarmed Tweed, and he made desperate attempts to stem the tide that was setting against him. At the Democratic State Convention, held in October, he received the nomination to the State Senate and his personal popularity in his district, where he had been bountiful in his gifts to the poor, assured his election. But he never took his seat. He was arrested October 26, 1871, in a civil action instituted by the Committee of Seventy and released on bail.

In December he was indicted for fraud and felony, and two weeks later he resigned his post as Commissioner of Public Works, ceasing about the same time to be the official head of Tammany Hall. He was brought to trial after many delays in January, 1873, but the ring still retained sufficient influence to secure a disagreement of the jury.

On a second trial in the following November he was convicted on fifty out of fifty-five charges against him and sentenced by Judge Davis to an aggregate of twelve years imprisonment. But at the end of the year, Tweed was released, the Court of Appeals holding that he could not begin to serve a new sentence of a year at the end of a term of service of punishment upon another count.

He was at once re-arrested upon civil actions to recover six million dollars stolen from the city, and being unable to obtain bail was kept in confinement in Ludlow Street jail. There he remained until December, 1875, when he effected his escape and was next heard of in Vigo, Spain. Here he was arrested and brought back in a Federal man-of-war and returned to jail. This was in November, 1876, and in the following March the city recovered judgment against him for $6,500,000. He could not pay. In April, 1878, he died in jail.

I have told this long story of Tweed in order that what follows, connecting him with Greenwich, may be more significant to the younger generation. And before I close this chapter it should appear that

Tweed, more than any other man of his time, fore-saw New York's imperial future.

It was at his initiative that, in 1868, the legislature chartered a company for the construction of a rapid transit subway on lines nearly identical with the lower half of the route now in operation, and in the same year he was instrumental in setting apart in Central Park a site for the present Metropolitan Museum of Art.

Credit must be given him for the establishment of fine floating baths, the Newsboys' Lodging House and the city's paid fire department, which has since become a model for the world. He did much to aid the extension and betterment of Central Park, and it is a matter of record that those who had the work in charge never appealed to him in vain for legislation or for funds.

No suspicion of fraud ever attached to this great undertaking, and it is said that Tweed ordered his followers to keep hands off the park. Another great work designed and accomplished by Tweed was the widening of Broadway from 32nd to 59th Street and the construction of what was long known as the Boulevard, but is now officially a section of Broadway, and which before its improvement was a narrow unpaved country road. He also led in the creation of the system of city-owned and improved water front, in which $60,000,000 is invested, and which has proved a boon to commerce and at the present time affords what is regarded by students of the subject as the most striking example offered here or abroad of profitable municipal ownership. "Tweed was not all bad," once declared the late Mayor William L. Strong. "He gave us the Boulevard, the annexed district, streets, parks, docks, schools and hospitals."

CHAPTER XVI

WILLIAM M. TWEED was a prominent character in Greenwich for a number of years. He took no part in the affairs of the town, but his presence was felt, with an effect very different on some than others. The sensible, well-bred men and women of the place greatly regretted his presence. They felt that the town could not grow in wealth and character, rendering Greenwich desirable as a place of residence so long as he remained to make it notorious.

It probably was true in those years that outsiders gave us a sneer when they alluded to Greenwich as the home of Tweed and the rendezvous of the Americus Club. But to the boys who admired his checkerboard team, his ponies and dog carts, he was an object of admiration. If they ever noticed Tom Nast's caricatures in *Harper's Weekly*, the purpose of such things was probably lost and as for reading all the papers said about him, detrimental to his reputation, they hardly took the pains. He was a living hero, with untold wealth, a great deal of which he dispensed locally with a liberal hand.

It is not certain whether he came here in 1860 or

WILLIAM M. TWEED

1861. The first knowledge that came to any of the village boys was that a number of tents were pitched on Round Island just south of the old potato cellar. And this fact left us in considerable uncertainty as to what the tents meant. It was the talk among the boatmen in the harbor and at Ephraim Read's on the steamboat dock that the tents were occupied by a club, but Tweed's name was not mentioned and it was not until the following summer that the name Americus Club was heard.

But Tweed had visited Greenwich during the first summer that the tents appeared. Certain members of the club, which afterwards became the Americus Club, had preceded him. This club was both social and political, being composed of Republicans and Democrats, although more of the latter prevailed than the former. I have never seen a list of the members during those early years of the club's existence, but I have a complete list of the membership of 1871, which was the most prosperous year in the club's history.

It was George E. Mann, Charles H. Hall and P. B. Van Arsdale who one day hired a sailboat at City Island and sailed up the Sound, with the expectation of returning before sunset. But the weather suddenly changed after they had left Execution Light far astern and rather than go about in the stiff southwest breeze that was blowing, they concluded to make a harbor for the night. Accordingly, they found good holding ground for the anchor under the lee

[181]

of Round Island and the tender took them ashore where they pitched a tent which they brought from the yacht.

The place was entirely new to them and they did not realize its beauty until the following morning. I have often heard Charles H. Hall tell of that next morning when the sun rose and revealed all the beauty of their surroundings.

Finch's Island, later known as Tweed's Island, had a beautiful grove of trees and its irregular shores

TWEED'S ISLAND, 1871

were not disfigured by sea walls. Captain's Island lighthouse was a short wooden affair to which was attached the diminutive home of the keeper. The same little house is now used as a summer kitchen and store room, the present stone building being erected in 1868. There was no fog horn then.

The more the young fellows looked around the better they liked the place and it was not until afternoon that they sailed for New York. Hall, who was afterwards secretary of the Americus Club, was one of the clerks in the Tombs Police Court. He was always a Republican, but he was a great favorite with

Mr. Tweed and as long as Tweed's influence lasted Charlie Hall had a lucrative place.

Mr. Tweed was foreman of the Big Six Volunteer Fire Co. with headquarters in an engine house on the Bowery. All the members of this company sooner or later were members of the Americus Club.

Tweed was accustomed to sit with the firemen around the engine house and he soon learned of the trip up the Sound and of the discovery made by his three mates. Their frequent allusion to the beauty of the spot finally caught Tweed's attention, with such force that he determined to investigate for himself.

Tweed and Hall took the train one afternoon consisting of an old wood-burning engine and yellow, gilt-trimmed cars, making the trip in the best time of those days, one hour and twenty minutes from 27th Street. They called on Oliver Mead, then owner of the property, and secured his permission to camp out on Round Island. They took possession a few days afterward and remained to the end of the season. They had two or three sailboats with enormous jibs and when they were not bathing on the beach or fishing or sailing, they were over at Rocky Neck.

The saloon on the point was an attraction as was Capt. Abraham Brinckerhoff's back dooryard, where they exchanged sea tales and discussed the merits of their boats by the hour. Later Captain Brinckerhoff and Mr. Tweed became very warm friends, and the latter gave the Captain many souvenirs and pictures, that constituted an interesting asset in his estate after his death. Among these are three photographs by A. Gurney, framed in black walnut and hanging at the present time in my office. One represents Indian Harbor from Tweed's Island, including the first club house built the year following the first camp on Round Island.

This building was of simple architecture, two

CAPT. BRINCKERHOFF
1816–1894

stories high, with a broad veranda. Painted under the peak of the roof in prominent black letters were the words "Americus Club of New York." It must have been about one hundred feet in width. On the first floor was a spacious reception room, a dining-room and a kitchen in the rear.

This house stood on the extremity of the point nearly in front of where Elias C. Benedict's house now stands. When the new house, which afterwards was known as the Morton House and later the Indian Harbor Hotel, was built, the old house was removed to a point in "Chimney Corner," now occupied by Mr. Benedict's boathouse. There it remained, somewhat altered and enlarged as the servants' quarters for the hotel until 1892 when it was torn down with all the other buildings on the Point.

AMERICUS CLUB HOUSE
Indian Harbor, 1862

WILLIAM M. TWEED

The other picture represents Mr. Tweed with the members of the club gathered about him on the rocks at the west side of the house and on the veranda; two groups of "the boys," as Tweed used to call them. It is quite easy to distinguish their features. The president of the club is dressed in a frock coat buttoned close about him. His hat is off, and a white necktie is beneath his chin. By his side stands Charles H. Hall, somewhat foppishly dressed in white trousers and dark coat. John and Dick Kimmons, great tall twins, and P. B. Van Arsdale are close to George E. Mann, who was Commodore in charge of the club fleet. These pictures were taken August 30, 1863.

The other picture that Captain Brinckerhoff had, was a quarter size India ink photograph of Mr. Tweed by the artist Brady, a famous war-time photographer. This picture was autographed but undated. It originally hung in the parlor of the new club house, and went into the possession of Capt. Brinckerhoff when the club broke up. John W. Delaney of this place now owns it.

In the original club house the Americus boys found their greatest enjoyment. It was more like a camp. The members appeared in their shirt sleeves, and lolled about on the rocks, or under the shade of the tall oaks, enjoying in the most unrestricted fashion their summer outing. Occasionally a visitor from the city or the village would appear, in which event Sec-

[187]

retary Hall would do the honors, with an old-fashioned cake basket and a little wine.

Sometimes the club members, in a body, would saunter up to the village, a very small collection of houses then, with a post office that paid the postmaster only $250 per annum. But when they did appear, with all sorts of pranks played upon each other and with jolly songs there was no one in the village that did not realize it, especially the children.

The new club house was completed in 1871 and stood on the point till the summer of 1892. It was three stories high, with a mansard roof, a tall tower, from which extended east and north two wings, terminating also in towers. It was a well-proportioned building, not architecturally bad, although the architect, Gage Inslee, had a lingering law suit in our courts in the endeavor to collect his fees. It occupied a commanding place on the point and, painted white, was a landmark for many miles up and down the Sound.

The summer of 1872 was the first season of its occupancy after its full completion. It had been furnished without regard to expense. The carpet in the great front room was woven abroad, one single piece, a hundred feet long, with tigers' heads in the corners and the center. A grinning tiger was the emblem of the club and Pottier & Stymus, who had big contracts for city furnishings, put the tiger's head upon every piece of furniture wherever it was possible.

But Mr. Tweed and his associates were never happy in this building. He had a grand room in the central tower, and Secretary Hall's suite was next, but in 1873 the revelations came and the place was abandoned as a club house. It was said that $105,000 was the expense of running the club that season.

Tweed's best enjoyment of his club was before

THE TWEED BATH HOUSE
Built 1870

1870. He was considered, in Greenwich, a very rich man and yet compared with the owners of the present-day fortunes, his circumstances were moderate. He was an extremely generous man, and indeed it has many times been said that had he not been anxious to enrich every one of his acquaintances no notice would have been taken of his irregularities. The amount he made out of the city contracts was small compared to the sums which went to his friends; and some whom he supposed were his friends were disloyal in the gloomy fall of 1873 when his arrest and indictment were accomplished.

DANIEL S. MEAD, Jr.
1840–1888

No man from Greenwich, however humble, ever went to that little office in Duane Street for help that he did not get it. If Mr. Tweed heard of a threatened foreclosure he bought the mortgage and collected such interest as the mortgagors found it convenient to pay. The Land Records show these transactions and they also show from time to time, Mr. Tweed took a deed of a small piece of property, which it was said the owners were unable to dispose of to any one else.

H. W. R. HOYT
State Senator 1869
1842–1894

Early in the summer of 1870, Mr. Tweed desired to have a family bathhouse and with that end in view he purchased on June 3, of Daniel S. Mead, three hundred and thirty-five feet of land on the easterly side of Rocky Neck harbor. The price he paid was $2,000.

On the mud flats south of the causeway to William

HEUSTED W. R. HOYT
As Judge of the Borough Court

WILLIAM M. TWEED

J. Smith's dock, he built an octagonal bath house, which was daily used by his family at high tide. The interior contained a bathing pool, the mud having been removed, and replaced by a large quantity of fine sand. Around this central pool were a number of rooms for the bathers, and it afforded a safe and secluded bathing place, approached by a wooden bridge from the shore. Mr. Tweed seldom, if ever, visited this house.

After the stress of hard times, on February 8, 1876, he sold this water front to Daniel S. Mead, Jr., a son of the original owner, for $1,000. The sale included the bathhouse which is said to have cost more than a thousand

H. W. R. HOYT
Age of 20

dollars. The house was subsequently moved to the shore and for a time was used as a dwelling. Later it was converted into an office for the Electric Light Co. and is now used by that company as a store room. The outward appearance of the building and its color remain the same, with the possible exception of an added cupola. Portions of this land which cost Tweed twenty-seven dollars a front foot, have since

[193]

been sold for about two hundred dollars per foot.

After Mr. Tweed was arrested in 1873 the late Col. Heusted W. R. Hoyt was his local counsel. William L. Ferris, a clerk in his office, made frequent trips to Ludlow Street jail in those days. Tweed occupied three splendidly furnished rooms on the ground floor. The first was a reception room covered with velvet carpet and supplied with luxurious couches and chairs. Adjoining was the business office where his private secretary, S. Foster Dewey, had his desk and beyond that was Mr. Tweed's bedroom.

PHILANDER BUTTON
1812–1878

Once when money seemed to be a little scarce with the old man, he brought out a large bundle of promissory notes, given by oyster men and mechanics, but the notes were of no value. "Well," said Mr. Tweed, "they had a value once. I had a lot of pleasure in taking them, when the money was needed."

It was in 1865, after he had established the Americus Club in their first house at Indian Harbor that Mr. Tweed became an actual resident of the village, although voting in New York. He bought of Lillie A. Hardenbrook what had been known as the Philander Button place. Mr. Button, who was the principal of the Greenwich Academy, had purchased it April 1, 1848, of Alvan Mead for $5,400. It included eighty acres, now a part of Milbank. He built a modest house on it and sold the building and forty acres, in January, 1859, to Mrs. Hardenbrook for $15,000. She sold it to Mr. Tweed's wife, Mary Jane Tweed, in 1865, for $18,000.

Mr. Tweed remodeled and enlarged the house and built a $40,000 barn that attracted a great deal of attention locally as well as in New York. The *New York Sun* sent up a reporter who described this wonderful barn and its contents, telling how the horses were standing on pleated straw. The barn remained in use till about 1907 when it was torn down.

DR. L. P. JONES
In 1884
1846–1907

Mr. Robert Williamson, the superintendent at Milbank, has told me that it was no easy matter to accomplish as the building was braced with hackmatack braces and trimmed with black walnut and other expensive wood.

Tweed was a lover of horses and he had some fine ones in his barn. His checkerboard four-in-hand team, to which I have already alluded, consisted of coal black and milk white horses, a black and white

[195]

and a white and black in alternating colors. They were driven to a very high two-seated depot wagon. The year 1867 was remarkable for the craze for high carriages.

Tweed occupied the back seat of this conveyance, with its enormously high springs. Usually his son was by his side, but his great weight of nearly three

hundred pounds gave the wagon a decided list. He generally wore a stove pipe hat and the closely buttoned frock coat and white tie. It was this rig which took him to the railroad station that summer morning in 1870 when he bought the eighteen acres of Frederick Mead.

JOSEPH G. MERRITT
1820–1885

E. Jay Edwards recently told this story in *The Evening Mail,* but I allude to it particularly because in some quarters it has been doubted and the assertion made that Mr. Mead never owned land east of what is now Milbank Avenue.

That street was a very narrow country road in those days, called Love Lane. It was never dignified with a proper street name until Mrs. Jeremiah Milbank generously put the Town Clock in the Congregational Church steeple and then Dr. Leander P. Jones had it changed to Milbank Avenue.

WILLIAM M. TWEED

In 1870 Frederick Mead owned eighteen acres directly across the street from the Congregational Church, bounded on the west by Love Lane and on the south by Davis Lane, now Davis Avenue. There were a few apple trees on it and at times Mr. Mead used it for pasture. It made a fine romping place for the Academy boys. Down at the south end was an old yellow barn, the front doors of which were locked with a padlock much larger than is made in these days. This lock made a fine target, although it was quite a long time before any one of the boys was able to put a bullet from a pistol through the keyhole of that lock. It was finally accomplished however and the back of the lock knocked off by a man now very well known in New York City, as a mining engineer.

Tweed had long wanted this land, and when Mr. Mead declined to put a price on it, Tweed said, "Well, you will take a Tweed price, will you not?" He had paid for several small places about town, anything that the owners demanded and when the price was large, as it always was, it had been usual to designate it as a "Tweed price." Tweed knew this and when he intimated that he was willing to pay a "Tweed price," he expected to pay more than the land was worth. In reply Mr. Mead said, "Why, yes, I'll sell for $55,000," which was at least four times the actual value of the land at that time. But it did not feaze Mr. Tweed. He asked Joseph G. Merritt, the ticket agent at the railroad station, for pen and ink and taking out a pocket check book he wrote a check for the amount to Mr. Mead's order and asked him to send him a deed conveying the property to Mary Jane Tweed. She held it until 1879, when it was included with all the rest of the Tweed place in the sale to Jeremiah Milbank for $47,500.

When Tweed bought this land the stone fence that enclosed it from the street was perhaps a century old, and somewhat out of order. He replaced it with the present bluestone wall, which extends from the property of A. Foster Higgins along Putnam Avenue, down Milbank Avenue to where the old yellow barn stood at the top of the hill across the road from the cemetery.

In those days the north end of Love Lane at its junction with Putnam Avenue turned with an angle to the west. When it was known that Mr. Tweed was about to build the new stone wall, Mr. Solomon Mead, a member of the Board of Burgesses, called upon him to see how much he would ask for a small angle of this valuable land to straighten the road. "Not a cent, not a cent," said Mr. Tweed. "Take all you want; just have your surveyor drive the stakes and I will build my wall according to his lines." And the wall stands there to-day just as perfect as when Mr. Tweed finished it, more than forty-two years ago.

Before I close this chapter it seems best to give the entire roll of members of the Americus Club in

WILLIAM M. TWEED

1871. Many of them besides Tweed were prominent and will be remembered by the older generation. Perhaps in no other way will this list be permanently preserved. The officers were William M. Tweed, 237 Broadway, President; Henry Smith, 300 Mulberry St., Vice President; Charles H. Hall, 135 Madison St., Secretary; George E. Mann, 197 Monroe St., Captain; John Vanderbeck, 221 Christie St., Actuary. Besides the officers were the following members: John S. Betts, Francis Vanderbeck, John McGarigal, P. B. Van Arsdale, William Davison, Lewis J. Kirk, Edward A. Davin, Lawrence Clancy, Francis Kinney, Edward Marrenner, William H. Schaffer, William B. Dunley, Joseph Southworth, John Scott, Edward J. Shandley, George W. Butt, James M. Macgregor, William L. Ely, Christian W. Schaffer, Walter Roche, Peter D. Braisted, Edward D. Bassford, Andrew J. Garvey, William K. O'Brien, George W. Rosevelt, Patrick H. Keenan, Joseph Shannon, James L. Miller, Terence Farley, Sheridan Shook, William H. Charlock, John T. Barnard, James Watson, Henry H. Huelat, Edward Boyle, William P. Stymus, John Pickford, Jr., Owen W. Brennan, Eugene Durnin, Charles G. Cornell, John J. Ford, Edwin M. Hagerty, Edward Hogan, Claudius S. Grafulla, Morgan Jones, Wesley S. Yard, John T. King, Edward Kearney, Joseph B. Young, Cornelius Corson, Robert M. Taylor, Edward Jones, Joseph A. Jackson, Amaziah D.

[199]

Barber, Charles L. Fleming, Jacob Sharp, Edward Cuddy, James O'Brien, John Satterlee, Andrew Bleakley, Thomas Donohoe, Martin B. Brown, Thomas E. Tripler, John T. McGowan, John Mc. B. Davidson, James H. Ingersoll, William C. Rogers, Sol. Sayles, Elbirt A. Woodward, George S. Miller, John H. Keyser, William C. Dewey, Daniel Berrien, David Miller, James Ryan, Michael J. Shandley, Isaac J. Oliver, Charles L. Lawrence, Henry D. Felter, John F. Chamberlain, James W. Boyle, Chris O'Connor, Kruseman van Elten, Daniel Winants, Alexander Frear, James Fisk, Jr., Jay Gould, Thomas Kirkpatrick, Joseph G. Harrison, Reeves E. Selmes, Charles E. Loew, Thomas C. Fields, George H. Mitchell, John Pyne, James J. Gumbleton, Thomas H. Ferris, Thos. J. O'Donohue, James E. Jones, John Garvey, James L. Harway, T. Augustus Phillips, John M. Carnochan, Matthew T. Brennan, James Barker, William B. Borrows, Henry A. Barnum, Schayler Halsey, James S. Watson, Newell Sturtevant, James W. Collier, Henry T. Helmbold, George A. Osgood, John Brice, Francis McCabe, John H. Harnett, James E. Coulter, Gunning S. Bedford, George G. Barnard, Andrew Bleakley, Jr., Augustus Funk, Peter Trainer, William Schirmer, Adolph E. Georgi, Joseph Koch, William Van Tassell, John Pentland, Thomas Canary, S. Foster Dewey, Dennis Burns, James McGowan, George G. Wolf, Frank S. E. Beck, Joseph D. C. Andrade, John D. Welch, Jr., Henry M. Wil-

WILLIAM M. TWEED

liams, Albert H. Wood, John W. Oliver, James
G. Dimond, George B. Van Brunt, Alex W. Harvey,
Richard O'Gorman, William Hitchman, Thomas J.
Creamer.

CHAPTER XVII

THE place, now known as Milbank, owned by
Mrs. A. A. Anderson, was the home of William
M. Tweed. The present property includes much
more territory, eighty acres being its extent, when it
was known as Linwood. Mr. Tweed was very proud
of the place and lavished money on it without stint.
The name Linwood seems to have been a favorite
of his, because he had a yacht of the same name and
the word was prominent on his stationery.

The yacht *Linwood* was a modest craft, possibly a
catboat. His big sailing yacht, a jib and mainsail
boat, bore the name of his wife, *Mary Jane Tweed*.
These boats, and indeed all the pleasure boats in the
harbor in those days, would not compare very favor-
ably with the boats of the present time. When it was
reported that Tweed had built a steam yacht, a good
deal of interest was manifest along the water front.
There may have been steam yachts long before, but
none had been in this harbor, at least not to remain
any length of time.

When she came steaming in from Northport where
she was launched, she was considered a wonder. Dr.
William Schirmer, Abraham Brinckerhoff, Simeon

Morrell and a string of the club members were on the steamboat dock as she came to an anchor. It seemed to me that none of them was very enthusiastic about her.

Her hull was shaped somewhat like an ocean-going tug, although only half the size of such a vessel. Her graceful mold was well-nigh destroyed in effect by the boxlike structure which made a large, high, and elegantly furnished cabin. She had side wheels, housed in like those of an old-fashioned ferryboat, and her name which was displayed on the pilot house in large gilt letters was that of the owner. Tweed took a great deal of comfort in his pioneer steam yacht.

In those days races among the oyster boats were common and regattas, in which those boats figured, were organized several times during the season. They were very fast jib and mainsail boats and often stowed below were balloon jibs and topsails that on occasion were run up to their places, when some other similar craft was showing a disposition to take the lead. There were no steamers then for oyster dredging and among the owners of these sailing vessels there was much rivalry. It was not limited to Greenwich oystermen, for these graceful little vessels came to join in the regattas from across the Sound. They came also from Norwalk, Five Mile River and Mamaroneck.

Nothing pleased Mr. Tweed better than to witness a race between these boats, and he always tendered his steam yacht for the use of the judges and the press. Of course that meant an elaborate spread in the cabin, with a lot of guests always eager to quench their thirst. While the yacht was homely, she was very comfortable, for the saloon was large, high and square. The table in the center on such occasions was loaded with all kinds of good things.

To a hungry youth—and what youth is not invariably hungry—these yacht races were memorable events. Plenty to see and plenty to eat, what experiences were they! And how well I recall the almost affectionate way in which Mr. Tweed would put his pudgy hand on my shoulder, with the remark, "Boy, did you get enough down below? Better go down and get another bird or a plate of whitebait." Of course he had no interest in me, except such feelings as any host possesses for a guest, but beyond that was his intense desire to stand well with the press. In a mixed crowd his first thought was for the newspaper representatives.

He had a great admiration and affection for Greenwich. He often steamed the yacht down to Jones' Stone and then back to the mouth of the Cos Cob harbor, and back again to Byram, all the while watching and commenting on the beauty of the shore.

One day he asked me to bring my camp stool near the capacious chair he occupied in the bow, and with a wave of his hand he directed my attention to all the wooded shore from Byram Point to Cos Cob, remarking: "I shall not live to see the day, but possibly you, and certainly your children, will see all this land occupied by the fine estates of New York business men. In my judgment Ochre Point at Newport is not as favorable for places of residence as Field Point and Nelson Bush's farm." The latter is now Belle Haven Park. Perhaps I looked incredulous, for he at once repeated the prophecy with emphasis and with just the suspicion of a shadow on his face he added: "When I am dead, say twenty-five years from now, I wish you would come out here and see how near I have hit it." He never lived to see his dream realized, but it came true in less time than he allotted.

His great hobby during those days was a daily steamboat to New York. He supposed that such an enterprise would yield a large pecuniary profit, and the subject was frequently on his lips, when aboard the yacht. He would call a few members of the club about him, and ask their opinion, none of whom knew anything more about it than he; yet he would seek from them information on the cost of coal, the probable number of passengers and the amount of freight likely to be carried. He exercised his own judgment finally, but he was led astray in this instance by his overweening desire to increase the popularity and the convenience of Indian Harbor.

While he could figure out in a moment the probable majority of a certain candidate in a city election, he had no idea of the possibility of the success or failure of such an enterprise. Indeed, it is probable that he had no anxiety on that point, provided he accomplished his purpose.

One day as we were sitting on the wide cane settee back of the pilot house Mr. Tweed appealed to Capt. Abe Brinckerhoff and I recall how the latter twisted the tobacco under his tongue and drawled out: "She won't earn the purser's salary, Mr. Tweed." The

latter looked quite crestfallen, and said, "Do you think so, Abe?" And that was all he did say for fully ten minutes except to order up some seltzer.

But as usual Mr. Tweed had his way, and he had a steamboat, the beautiful *John Romer*. She was a very fast boat

T. F. SECOR
1809–1901

and she did not end her career until the middle eighties when she was on the line between Boston, Hingham, Hull and Nantasket.

He talked about his plans, as they matured. He was very particular about a bartender, and eventually he selected just the right man as well as excellent officers for the steamer.

The *Romer* came from Wilmington, Del. She was built by the famous firm of Harlan & Hollingsworth and was supplied with Allaire engines. The Allaire Engine Co. built most of the marine engines installed immediately after the war. The president of the Allaire Co. was Theodocius F. Secor, who resided on Lake Avenue for many years and died April 27, 1901, at the age of 92. His widow still lives here.

The *Romer's* furnishings were luxurious and her speed was greater than most boats of her length and tonnage. The price asked was $50,000, but her owners were pecuniarily embarrassed and Mr. Tweed got her for $35,000—a great bargain. He was never known to haggle at a price, and doubtless some of the officers of the corporation known as the Greenwich & Rye Steam-

CAPT. THOMAS MAYO
1819–1887

boat Co. should have the credit of making the purchase.

This corporation was formed early in 1866. Capt. Thomas Mayo, whose daughters still reside here, was elected its president, and Sanford Mead, secretary. Subsequently Philander Button, then principal of the Academy, occupied the position of president. The capital stock was $75,000, of which $70,000 was paid in, one-half of which went for the purchase of the *Romer*. Mr. Tweed held 200 shares, par value $100, and members of the Americus Club held a sufficient number, with Mr. Tweed, to control the company. The balance of the stock was held in small lots in Greenwich and Port Chester.

The boat was decidedly popular, as is evident from the fact that her gross earnings the first year were $21,763.15, expenses $21,417.28, leaving a net balance of only $345.87. This small amount was kept

SANFORD MEAD
1803–1873

as a reserve fund to disappear the following year in financial chaos. The summer of 1867 was the last of the *Romer* in these waters.

In passing, I must recall two of her officers— Captain Stephen G. White and the pilot, Billy Witherwax. Capt. White had had experience as a steamboat captain on the Pacific Coast, and he made an efficient and popular commander. He was a round, jolly man with a merry laugh, the ring of which I well remember. His son, Warren P. White, is a resident of Greenwich, as is also his daughter, Mrs. Lucy M. Delano.

Pilot Witherwax had been commander and part owner of a sky-sail yard flyer, that had successfully rounded Cape Horn so many times that he was worth $50,000—a snug fortune for those days. He had retired from the sea when Mr. Tweed met him and he consented to take a position on the *Romer* as a favor to Mr. Tweed. He was a typical sailor. His square built form had the power of an ox, while his sphinx-like face recalls the former Vice-President of the United States, William A. Wheeler.

To make the boat popular, the company resorted to every legitimate means to introduce her to the public. With this end in view a grand Fourth of July excursion to New Haven, with Dodworth's band in attendance, was announced in 1867. The proposed trip was the talk of the town, and when on that beautiful summer morning, the order was given to cast off the lines, the boat was loaded with a

STEPHEN G. WHITE
1826–1881

party decidedly miscellaneous in its make-up, but evidently happy and bent on having a good time.

As we passed Red Rock, I remember well how Capt. White stood forward, chewing an unlighted cigar and congratulating everybody on the beauty of the morning. But Billy Witherwax was unusually glum and once as I met him aside from the crowd, he significantly remarked, "Capt. White likes

[209]

this weather, but I don't. Look out for a blow when the tide turns." I inquired why he thought so, and he replied, "Mares' tails to the s'uth'ard!" and diving into the pilot house closed the door.

Everything went well until after we left New Haven to return. I had forgotten Pilot Witherwax's remark about the mares' tails, when I suddenly became conscious of the fact that the wind was freshening and that the sky was becoming overcast. Ladies were sending for extra wraps and there was a general disposition to seek the seclusion of the cabin. Inside, the roll of the vessel became more perceptible; a general complaint concerning the closeness of the atmosphere was heard and then followed a stampede for the deck. The storm had arisen with great suddenness, and as the passengers came out, many of them were drenched with flying spray. The boat rolled terribly, and the noise of the guards striking the water as she lay in the trough of the sea struck terror to the now thoroughly frightened excursionists. Two lunch counters and a liberally stocked bar had been well patronized all the morning. In the tumult of the angry elements there seemed to be universal nausea attributable in part to the choppy sea and in part to the conviviality of the forenoon.

Under the circumstances two hundred and fifty people found it necessary to visit the boat's rail and as the wind was blowing a gale, broadside on, the seasick excursionists found the weather rail unsatisfactory.

They all, therefore, with one accord sought the lee rail and there endeavored to relieve their sufferings. As the steamer was three decks high, two-thirds of the passengers suffered intensely from their location and the only clean hats, coats and bonnets were in possession of those who occupied the upper deck. No sicker, sorrier or more dejected set of human beings ever landed in Port Chester than those who, late that night, went ashore from the *Romer*. It was deemed unsafe to land at Greenwich.

Many of the present generation have never heard of this sea trip because those of the older generation hate to think of it, and never speak of it.

There is one other incident in connection with the *Romer* that I cannot omit. Greenwich has always been interested in temperance, if one may judge from the societies and legions which have usually existed here. In 1866 that famous but erratic man, William H. H. Murray, was the preacher at the Second Congregational Church. He was a strong advocate of temperance. He rejoiced over the new steamboat, but when he was told that a bar was to be maintained he predicted the failure of the enterprise. It was his wish that the boat should be run without a bar, and in a quiet way he made every effort to have his wish complied with. The stock list showed a large number of Congregationalists who doubtless would have been glad to have no bar, but the Tweed stock controlled and the bar was an established fact. Sanford Mead made every endeavor to keep out the bar.

Mr. Murray, however, was not satisfied. He believed that it was his duty to preach against that bar, even if some of the company's directors did occupy prominent pews in his church. Accordingly, the sermon was announced a week in advance and the church was crowded. I cannot recall the text, nor can I remember much about the sermon. There was, however, one exclamation from the preacher that I have never forgotten. He alluded to the fact that excuses had been made for the existence of the bar and that one of the officers had informed him that it was "out of sight; way down below." Then shaking his black locks from his forehead in that tragic way so common to him he added: "And, brethren, so is hell, way down below!" Four years after that memorable sermon was delivered, Murray was the pastor of the Park Street Church, in Boston, and the *John Romer* was running from Rowe's Wharf in the same city to Hull, Hingham and Nantasket.

As I have said, the *Romer* was a boat of great speed and no steamer of her size going out of the port of New York could overhaul her. The *Seawanhaka* was a fine boat running to Sea Cliff. She was twice the size of the *Romer,* with engines of enormous power for a small boat, and equally well manned and officered. She represented the wealth of

Roslyn and Sea Cliff and was launched early in 1866. The claim was freely made that her speed would exceed that of any other steamer on the Sound.

The *Romer* had always been able to take the lead on the run from her berth to Execution Light, and it struck Capt. White and Billy Witherwax rather hard to think of giving up their laurels. For a time they managed to keep out of the *Seawanhaka's* way, but finally on the second day of June, 1867, it was apparent to all on board that a race was inevitable. One of the officers of the *Romer* gave me this account of the affair:

"We had three-quarters of an hour's start of the "*Seawanhaka,* but as we approached Throgg's Neck "we could see her astern, gaining rapidly. Pilot "Witherwax was at the wheel and Capt. White "stood aft with a pair of glasses watching the on-"coming steamer. Every two or three minutes With-"erwax would ring for more steam, till at last John "Darrah, the engineer, called through the speaking "tube that he was doing all he could and that it was "useless to keep ringing, as the throttle was wide open "and there was no more steam to be had. 'Well, "make more steam,' was Witherwax's reply; in re-"sponse to which I heard the engineer groan as "though the task imposed upon him was hopeless.

"It was evident that the pilot intended, if possible, "to keep the lead until he could reach the narrow "channel between Riker's Island and Barrow's Point, "for beyond that he thought that once ahead of the

"*Seawanhaka* he could maintain his position for
"the balance of the trip. The intense interest in the
"pilot house and the engine room amounted to ex-
"citement among the passengers and many bets were
"made on the result. Some of the Americus Club
"boys on the quarter deck became hilarious and the
"secretary of the Steamboat Co., who happened to be
"aboard, went to the bartender and said, 'Now
"Henry, I wish you would go a little easy with the
"boys.' 'Why, what do you mean, Mr. Mead?' said
"Henry. 'Well, I mean,' was the reply, 'that while
"this race lasts you must give the boys sarsaparilla
"when they ask for whisky, and if they call for
"brandy, make it a point to serve seltzer.' Henry
"smiled at the idea of thus fooling an Americus Club
"man but nevertheless he promised to try it.

"But to return to the race. Pilot Witherwax had
"calculated correctly, for he succeeded in getting
"abreast of North Brother Island before the *Seawan-
"haka* began to lap over the *Romer*. At this point
"she was slipping by at the rate of about ten feet a
"minute, guard to guard, with the *Romer* so close
"that conversation was easily carried on between the
"two vessels.

"The passengers and crews of both boats were now
"in a fever heat of excitement.

"I think I never saw such a crazy lot as yelled at
"each other across the span of a dozen feet between
"the two boats. Women shook their parasols in the
"air and squealed like a flock of geese.

"Billy Witherwax's face was as stern as an In-
"dian's. Again he gave the bell for more steam only
"to be disappointed. Every minute made a decided
"difference in the relative position of the contending
"steamers, and it was plain that something more must
"be done, and without delay, or the *Romer* would be
"left behind.

"Witherwax again sought the tube and yelled:
" 'Give her more fire. If you can't find anything
"else throw Pat. Donnelly into the furnace. We
"must have more fire, and I guess he'll burn.'

"Patrick Donnelly, only recently deceased, then
"occupied a responsible position on the quarter deck
"of the *Romer*. He knew all about the freight and
"how it was stowed. He knew exactly where to put
"his hand on a tub of Abe Acker's lard and when
"he heard the order repeated by the engineer, rather
"than be sacrificed himself, he produced the lard.
"The fireman seized it and flung it on the coals. The
"steamer leaped ahead like a sailboat in a squall.
"Black smoke belched from the stack. She walked
"by the *Seawanhaka* as the *Pilgrim* will pass the
"*Sarah Thorp*.

"Witherwax's triumph was complete and he held
"the *Romer* on her course in an undisputed lead all
"the way to Twenty-third Street."

The *Seawanhaka* never bothered the *Romer* again,
but I never pass the "sunken meadows" and see the
ghostly hog frame of the lost *Seawanhaka* rising
amid the swaying drift of sedge grass that I do not

recall the fact that the 2nd June, 1880, when she was driven onto those meadows, wreathed in flames, was the thirteenth anniversary of her famous race with the *John Romer*.

CHAPTER XVIII

THE TWEED FAMILY

THE members of Mr. Tweed's family were well known about the village. While many of the villagers treated them with something like an air of awe, they mixed in quite well and those who knew them liked them.

The oldest son was William M., Jr. We knew him as "Billy" and he was quite intimate with Henry M. FitzGerald and Stephen G. White.

Billy Tweed was a fine-looking young man in those days. He was tall and straight, carried himself well, and wore Dundreary whiskers. If a man could raise a good pair of "side-boards," as such whiskers were called, he was all right. And this Billy had done to perfection.

It is somewhat singular that William M. Tweed, Jr., married a Greenwich girl whom he met in New York City. Her father and many earlier generations were natives of the town and lived at Davis Landing. Her father was Silas Davis, who for many years was engaged in the flour business in New York under the firm name of Davis & Benson. He had made a large fortune and his daughter had all the advantages afforded by wealth. She was then a beautiful girl of fine character and she is still a handsome woman, upon whom the hand of time has rested lightly. Her husband died about 1908.

The next son was Richard. He had a very fast black horse that he drove at top speed from Maple Avenue to Putnam Hill. It was his habit to do this nearly every day, till the warden of the Borough put a stop to it by telling Dick that if he wanted to trot his horse, he had better enter him at Jerome Park. Richard went to Europe in 1879, subsequently married the widow of his brother Charles and shortly afterward died in Paris.

There were two daughters whose names I do not recall. They married two wealthy brothers by the name of McGuinness who resided in New Orleans and there they went to live about 1871. I am told that one is still living and moves in the best circles of that aristocratic southern city.

Josephine came next. She was a young lady of great beauty, a brunette, and was about eighteen years old when her father was at the height of his glory. She drove a pair of beautifully matched, high-spirited black horses. It was certainly a pleasure to observe the skill and dignity with which she would rein the team up in front of the post office for the afternoon mail. She married a wealthy New Yorker by the name of Frederick Douglas and in 1898 they were living on Staten Island.

Jennie was a school girl in 1865 and was thus well known by the school children of that period. Hers was a short life, as she died before she was twenty.

Charlie was a romping boy in his early teens, with a lively pony and without much time for his books. School had little attraction for him and at one time he had a tutor. Had he lived in these days he would have possessed a high power motor car, if not a flying machine. But everybody liked Charlie Tweed and all were saddened at the news of his death some years after Linwood was sold.

George was a baby in 1865. Of him I never had a very intimate knowledge, as he died in early youth.

After Tweed's troubles began in 1873, the glory of Linwood began to wane. The checkerboard team was seen no more and many of the other fine horses were sold. Money ceased to flow in, and after the incarceration in Ludlow Street jail, the demands that were made upon Tweed by his lawyers for a defense fund were large. John Graham, bewigged and always wearing kid gloves with the fingers amputated, was his chief counsel. Elihu Root, now so well known, was at the head of a younger coterie of men who worked up the details of the defense that did not succeed.

All this required large sums of money and from time to time various things were sold at Linwood. The greenhouses were stripped of rare plants and many articles that had special value because of their association, were quietly disposed of for a substantial consideration. When Greenwich Avenue was recently widened at its lower end, on what was formerly the Thomas Ritch property, I saw a couple of ornate iron lamp posts pulled down that formerly stood in front of the house at Linwood. There were many other things that found their way into the possession of Greenwich people who afterwards would sometimes covertly allude to their origin.

By this it must not be inferred that the family was impoverished. Mrs. Tweed owned valuable real es-

FRANK SHEPARD
In 1869

tate here and in New York City and it was probably only because of a desire to limit expenses and prepare for the final disposition of Linwood that she made such disposition of her personalty. The property was listed with many real estate agencies in New York City and was brought to the attention of many local capitalists, but it remained unsold year after year, when the price asked for eighty acres was only fifty thousand dollars.

Finally in the fall of 1878 a syndicate was formed consisting of A. Foster Higgins, Solomon Mead, Frank Shepard, principal of the Academy, and one or two others, whose names I do not recall. To one of the syndicate, whose name is not mentioned, was entrusted the duty of closing the deal.

The purpose of the syndicate was to establish a residence park, something like Rockefeller Park, although the demand for house lots was not as active in those days as it was after the public water and sewers had been introduced. It would have made, however, an ideal residence park and it was the pioneer effort in that direction. The matter dragged along through the winter months of 1878, without any report to the syndicate, and finally in February, 1879, its members awoke to the fact that the land had slipped away from them and had become the property of Jeremiah Milbank, having sold for $47,500.

When the title was being closed in the old Town Clerk's office I asked William M. Tweed, Jr., who represented his mother, how it happened that the $50,000 offer was rejected. "No such an offer was made," said he. "I would have been glad of $2,500 more, but the offer that came to me from the syndicate was $40,000 and I was told that no better offer would be made." It was just one of those little incidents, growing out of lack of judgment, probably, that often attend real estate transactions and are far-reaching in their consequences.

In 1868 and 1869 Mr. Tweed was in the height of his glory. He ruled New York with an iron hand and yet there must have been times when he realized that his political power rested on a thin shell of corruption, liable any day to collapse and plunge him into a vortex of adverse public sentiment. He loved flattery and he hated to be criticised. Tom Nast, Harpers' famous cartoonist, had even then sharpened his pencil and occasionally Tweed appeared in the

Weekly with a blazing diamond in his shirt front. But nothing in those years appeared that seemed serious to Tweed, although they greatly annoyed him.

As an offset to such influences, Senator Harry Genet and a few of that ilk started a general contribution to a fund for a public statue to Mr. Tweed, to be erected in Central Park. These men realized what many people have failed to give Mr. Tweed credit for, and that was his remarkable conception of the future of the City of New York. He often expressed regret that Manhattan Island with its magnificent water front, should have been laid out in angles and squares, and it was he who planned the Boulevard and Riverside Drive.

During this period he cast about for sustaining influences and in the summer of 1868 and 1869 he invited the children of the city orphan asylum on Randall's Island to visit him at Linwood. They were called for short the "Randall's Island children," and their coming was announced several days in advance. Dodworth's band—Tweed would have nothing else—came with them on a steamboat chartered for the occasion. They were marched up Greenwich Avenue and down Putnam Avenue to Linwood, with the band in advance and most of the villagers looking on with pride at the benevolent act of their distinguished neighbor. Mr. Tweed in his silk hat and frock coat with the inevitable white tie, stood out on the lawn in front of the house and reviewed his youthful guests; on one occasion addressing them as the future voters of the great metropolis. After this ceremony they disbanded, with evident relief, and were turned loose on the Linwood grounds, to the great disgust of Theodore H. Mead, whose apple orchard adjoined and suffered accordingly.

Perhaps it was the same spirit of assumed benevolence that caused him to donate to one of the village churches a sandstone baptistry around the base of which was inscribed, with letters deeply cut, the words, "The gift of William M. Tweed, 1869." It still remains within the church, although it has lost its former place of prominence.

During this period he was also recognized as generous to the bearer of a subscription paper and the object mattered not; black or white, Catholic or Protestant, all were received with a benign smile and a ready response.

On one occasion the good ladies of a certain religious organization called upon him with the request for a subscription for an organ. Before approaching him, however, they had gathered up all the subscriptions possible, but had found rather hard sledding, with the result that the pledges were only half sufficient.

Taking the subscription paper, he footed up the various small amounts, with the stub of a pencil he had taken from his vest pocket, and looking over his gold-rimmed glasses at the somewhat awed committee, he said, "Well, what is the damn thing going to cost, anyway?"

The ladies were shocked at the expression, but a quickly drawn check for the balance required, served as a relief for their feelings, and they left expressing many thanks and a world of good wishes.

CHAPTER XIX

IN Chapter XV allusion has been made to the escape of Tweed from jail and his subsequent apprehension and arrest in Vigo, Spain. One of his own appointees in the Sheriff's office took him out for a ride; he stopped to make a call at his own home in the city, and he never appeared again until several months had elapsed. Many accounts have been given of his escape and of his place of hiding before he embarked for Spain, but all of them are very far from the truth.

Before I relate the actual story of his escape, let me recall certain facts, within the memory of many Greenwich people, which are closely connected with that event.

On the ninth day of June, 1870, one Isaac Mosher sold twenty-four acres of land and a farm house northwest of Cos Cob village to Lydia G. McMullen, the wife of William McMullen. The price paid was $12,300 and the transaction was closed in the office of Col. Heusted W. R. Hoyt, counsel for Mr. Tweed. The latter was present on the occasion and subsequently he gave a great deal of attention to the improvements made to the property. This place is located on the easterly side of the highway running northerly from the Post Road near the residence of Augustus and Catherine Mead which was then known as the Edward Mead homestead. The house is still standing, but since the days of Tweed has been much enlarged and more recently has been known as the Ardendale Sanitarium. He introduced Mrs. McMullen as his niece and it was understood that she and her husband were, to a certain extent, dependent upon him.

Andrew J. Garvey, a member of the Americus Club, and generally known, from his numerous contracts, as the city plasterer, paid all the repair bills on the McMullen house. Garvey usually left the train at Cos Cob carrying a carpetbag filled with greenbacks with which to pay the mechanics and material men employed on the job. Subsequently in one of the ring prosecutions in the New York Supreme Court, the fact appeared that, at least the plastering, if not all of the repair work on the McMullen house, was charged to the city.

At that period the Cos Cob station agent was a young man who has since been a prominent resident and officeholder in the Borough. He had considerable to do with handling the freight and express packages for the McMullen house, to his pecuniary advantage, and after the family moved in, he continued to be a great favorite with them because of his universal courtesy and promptness.

On his home trip from the Duane Street office in

New York, Mr. Tweed usually left the train at Greenwich, but, as he held in high esteem his nephew and niece, it is not strange that occasionally he was invited to pass the night with them at Cos Cob.

The young station agent began to notice that the 9.15 evening train at Cos Cob would frequently stop a thousand feet west of the station, down by Edward Mead's bars, and then crawl up to the station. In the glare of the headlight it was hard to determine why the pause was made, as down the length of the train was impenetrable darkness. Frank Hermance was the conductor of the train. He was one of the old-fashioned conductors, who carried a lantern with his name ground on the glass globe and a rose in his buttonhole. When he entered the door he came with a bound and a smile and many will recall how he purred the words, "Good morning, brother," as he punched the tickets.

It was the duty of the station agent to report such an irregularity as halting a train down by Edward Mead's bars and especially when the occurrence was frequent. Finally he told Mr. Hermance that he would be obliged to report him if it occurred again, but Frank only smiled and gave the station agent a friendly salute as he started his train.

About this time Tweed was indicted by the Grand Jury of New York County, locked up in the Tombs and upon the trial before Judge Noah Davis and a jury was convicted. Judge Davis had never been a friend of Tweed's and on the opening day of the trial, John Graham, his leading counsel, very humbly suggested that His Honor "was disqualified," for which insinuation Mr. Graham was promptly fined $250. But the charge to the jury was fair and the only criticism counsel for the defense made was "the remarkable sentence imposed by the Court."

He was convicted on fifty out of fifty-five charges against him and sentenced by Judge Davis to an aggregate of twelve years imprisonment. He might have been sentenced for sixty years, but Judge Davis decided that he would give him a sentence proportionate to his average share in the stealings; that is that he would give him twenty per cent. of what he might have imposed upon him.

Then the question was generally discussed as to whether a cumulative sentence, as it was called, was legal. Graham appealed to the General Term, now called the Appellate Division, and was defeated, but afterwards the Court of Appeals held that Tweed could not begin to serve a new sentence of a year at the end of a term of service of punishment upon another count.

Meanwhile Tweed went to Blackwell's Island and began to serve his sentence, occupying a double room luxuriously furnished, near the northeast end of the penitentiary building. In going down the East River, on the Brooklyn side you may still see in the grim walls of the great building a double window, the only one, which was made expressly to add to the comfort of Mr. Tweed in his days of imprisonment, when he was being attended by the officers who owed their appointment to their prisoner.

Upon the reversal of the judgment by the Court of Appeals Mr. Tweed was re-arrested and held in Ludlow Street jail under the civil suit brought by the city for six million dollars damages and it was from this place that one night he made his escape.

It is unnecessary here to go into the particulars of that escape further than as they are connected with and apply to the town of Greenwich. Tweed had disappeared and there was no clew to his whereabouts. Andrew H. Green, Charles O'Conor, Joseph H. Choate and the others of the famous Committee of Seventy offered a reward of fifty thousand dollars for his apprehension. If you will read the newspapers of those days you will notice that from the time of his departure till he was reported in Vigo, Spain, there is no positive account of his whereabouts. There were at least two men, however, who might have made the story clear. One was the young station agent at Cos Cob and the other was George W. Hoffman.

It was in the early winter of 1875 that the Cos Cob agent, who had just laid aside an evening paper telling of the escape of Tweed and advertising the fifty-thousand dollar reward notice, that the 9.15 train again made its mysterious stop at Edward Mead's bars. The agent was angry. The conductor had disregarded his threat to report him, and was again disobeying the rules. Seizing a lantern he ran down the track. As he passed beyond the glare of the headlight and reached the baggage car, he saw the side door slide open. At that moment a woman from behind smashed his lantern. Bewildered in the sudden darkness, he stepped forward and put his hand on the great bulk of William M. Tweed. There was a man with him and a woman followed, leaping

across the ditch beside the track, and up the bank through Edward Mead's bars. There a carriage was in waiting and George W. Hoffman was on the box.

Who was Hoffman? He was not a member of the Americus Club and I could never get any definite information as to who he was, except that Philip N. Jackson, the son of an Americus Club man, said he was one of Tweed's men. Jackson was a messenger in the New York Supreme Court by Tweed's appointment and in the late seventies and early eighties was the trial justice in Greenwich.

JAMES ELPHICK
1824—1889

After Tweed's death Hoffman came to Greenwich to reside. He apparently had considerable money and he purchased of James Elphick a large area of oyster ground. A long and serious litigation then followed between Elphick and Hoffman over the contracts for the purchase of this oyster ground, and the case finally terminated in the Court of Errors in favor of Mr. Elphick and is reported in the 49th volume of Connecticut Reports.

While this litigation was in progress, I saw much of Hoffman and on more than one occasion he admitted that Tweed came up on the 9.15 on the night in question, occupying the baggage car. Hoffman never told how he got Tweed into the car at 42nd Street, but at that time there was ample opportunity to walk, unseen, down what had once been Fourth Avenue, on the south side of the train and slip into the baggage car.

From Cos Cob the carriage, with Tweed in it, was driven to the McMullen house, where his last meal in Greenwich was eaten. Thence he was driven across to Tarrytown where a tug chartered by Hoffman was waiting. This tug took Mr. Tweed down to the lower bay and to an outgoing freight steamer bound for Cuba.

In the port of Havana under the beetling walls of Moro Castle Tweed was transferred to another steamer bound for Spain and was subsequently captured at Vigo and sent back to Ludlow Street jail where he died April 12, 1878, at the age of fifty-five.

Often I have thought of that $50,000 reward that the young station agent made no attempt to earn. How easy it would have been to telegraph the authorities who had offered the reward, and to have caught Tweed that night as his last dinner in the McMullen house was being served. The agent knew exactly where he was. He was poor then, but now he is worth more than twice the amount of that reward. Once I asked him about it. He took from his lips an expensive cigar and contemplated reflectively its long, unbroken ash. Then he looked at me and said, "I thought of it, but how could I?"

CHAPTER XX

THE old Town Hall, which stood where the Soldiers' Monument now stands, was burned the night of October 15, 1874. This building had been used many years for public meetings, theatrical shows, church fairs, elections, and as a court room for the trial Justice of the Peace.

It was a single room, lighted by eight windows, containing a portable bench for the court and an enclosure for the lawyers, which usually stood on the east side of the room. The Selectmen and other town officials had their offices in a small frame building, on Greenwich Avenue, which stood where the brick building of Tuthill Brothers now stands. At a later date the officials occupied rooms in the old Congregational Church building after it was removed to the corner of Putnam Avenue and Sherwood Place.

At the time of the fire it had outlived its usefulness. As early as 1873 the question of a new town hall was seriously considered. At the annual meeting in that year, Luke A. Lockwood, Drake Mead, William J. Mead, Odle C. Knapp and Thomas A. Mead were appointed to inquire into the expediency of erecting a new building. This committee was also

[233]

charged with the duty of recommending the location, the size, architectural character and internal arrangement of such a building, and the estimated cost.

The following year the committee was continued,

TOWN HALL
Drawn from description by Carleton W. Hubbard

having reported progress. A set of plans had been prepared for a building which was to be erected on the northeast corner of Putnam Avenue and Sherwood Place, then considered the business center. These plans were afterwards framed and for many years hung on the wall of the Town Clerk's office.

Mr. George Jackson Smith, the Town Clerk at that time, had a habit of boasting of his expensive

[234]

wall decoration, for the picture cost the town twelve hundred dollars.

It would seem, however, that many were interested in the subject and desirous of carrying out the plans, because in 1874 the Selectmen were authorized to apply to the General Assembly for authority to bond the town for $75,000, for the purpose of building a new town hall. A spe-

cial town meeting was called November 28, 1878, and the Town Hall Committee was instructed to present plans and make report to a "special meeting hereafter to be called to consider the whole subject of a new Town Hall."

GEORGE J. SMITH
1814–1877

While the new Town Hall was being discussed, the officials moved into Aaron P. Ferris' new building, which had been erected for a hotel and is the building now owned by the town and occupied by Mayer H. Cohen.

The town paid an annual rent of $600. The Selectmen occupied the south side and the Town Clerk and Judge of Probate the north side, first floor. The second and third floors were occupied as tenements until the first of July, 1875, when the second floor was converted into public offices. Myron L. Mason,

OTHER DAYS IN GREENWICH

Edward J. Wright, Charles Cameron, Leander P. Jones, M.D., Dr. Beverly E. Mead, R. Jay Walsh, James F. Walsh, Frederick A. Hubbard and possibly others occupied offices on the second floor of this building.

TOWN HALL IN 1878
John H. Ray and John E. Ray stand in the foreground under the tree planted by Edward J. Wright

It was crowded, uncomfortable and badly arranged for such purposes and yet for years it was the only place for an office because it was the actual business center. The Assessors, Board of Relief and Tax Collector all found places wherever they could, unless actually excluded by a justice trial, held in the Selectmen's office.

[236]

THE OLD TOWN HALL

But the scheme to build a new town hall was forgotten and we might still be using the Aaron P. Ferris building, but for the liberality of the late Robert M. Bruce who, with his sister, Miss Sarah Bruce, donated the new building.

ROBERT M. BRUCE
Philanthropist
Besides many other benevolent gifts, donated to Greenwich its Town Hall, Public Park and Hospital

On May 15, 1875, Mr. Ferris made a written proposition to sell his building to the town. He described the property as 50 feet wide and 254 feet deep and the price named was $11,500, to be paid in a series of notes, drawing interest at the rate of seven per cent., payable over a term of ten years. The proposition was accepted at a special town meeting and the town took title and still owns the property; the front half of which yields a rental of about twelve hundred dollars a year and reserves shed room in the rear.

At the time the town took title we had no public water, sewers or lights. The water supply for the town building was a large well, which was filled up in 1896. But the occupants of the building realized its unsanitary condition and at the annual town meeting in 1878 the Town Clerk and the Judge of Probate were appointed a committee "whose duty it shall be, at an expense not exceeding $300, to make needed repairs and improvements in and about the rear of the town building, for the purpose of proper use and protection of the well; to effect safe and convenient exit from the rear doors of the building; to build a cistern for the use of the tenants and as a provision against fire." At the same meeting it was voted to build a lockup and it is still standing as a storage room in the rear of Cohen's store.

But for seventeen years matters went on in this way without a ripple until September 9, 1895, when an attempt was made to purchase the land adjoining on the south owned by Mary F. Dayton and now occupied by Elias S. Peck. It was thought that the lot enlarged to a width of 100 feet would warrant the town in tearing down the old building and erecting a new town hall about fifty feet back from the street, with light on all sides. But the proposition was voted down and we struggled on under the old conditions until January 1, 1906, when the new town hall was occupied.

Both of these old town buildings are of peculiar interest. The first one was probably built about 1830 and represented a building typical of the rural, farming people. The illustration which is given is made from a description of the building, there being no photograph of it in existence. But the drawing so accurately illustrates the old building that those of the older generation will at once recognize it. During all those fervid times before and during the war of 1861 it was used as a polling place, as indeed it was up to the time of its destruction. But in the war time it was the place of many an angry debate and many incidents occurred which are still talked about.

Two very estimable and prominent neighbors once got into a hot political dispute on an election day. One resisted the entrance of the other, through the door, with the result that one of the doors was pulled off the hinges and the two contestants with the door rolled down the hill.

From 1854 till long after the war the Borough meetings were held in the old town hall, but the Burgesses met at private houses and usually at the home of the Clerk.

I first knew of Borough meetings in 1860. Billy Trumble, a quaint little old man, was the town janitor. For a number of years he had been man of all work for the Rev. Dr. Joel H. Linsley, and, holding such a post, he fancied he knew all the affairs of the parish.

The old man had quite an attraction for me and his sterling character and odd sayings made their impression. It was his duty to open and light the hall for the annual meetings of the Borough.

After he had arranged the benches and dusted the chairs, he would take his seat and with the immense brass door key across his lap await the coming of the Warden.

On such occasions I enjoyed sitting by his side and listening to the queer stories of what he claimed to have seen and heard around the old white church, then standing in front of the present stone edifice. I was only a small boy, but I realize how the old man enjoyed impressing upon my youthful fancy his visits at night to the pulpit and the pews, where he routed out the bats that were circling around in the moonlight.

In those days the workmen were busy on the new church and piles of rubbish and blocks of cut stone occupied every possible place about the town hall. The cellar had also been invaded by the stonecutters and it was a weird place at night after they had abandoned it to the darkness and the bats. One of Billy's duties was to gather up the chisels and hammers which the workmen had carelessly left, and as his "chores" at the parsonage, as he called his small errands about the place, often kept him till his lantern was needed, it was my great delight to go with him on such nocturnal trips, poking about among the chips for the stray tools.

But nothing was more agreeable to Billy than the occasion of the annual Borough meeting. I think he felt quite as important as the Warden and he was certainly better paid, as that official drew no salary.

After the arrival of the Warden the next man to appear was Robert W. Mead, the clerk. These officials would talk a few minutes, but no one else appearing, the Warden would step over to the parsonage, while the clerk would hurry up to Solomon Mead's and Charles H. Seaman's, and Billy, while I tagged at his heels, would be sent down to invite Henry M.

AMOS M. BRUSH
In 1860
1825–1905

Benedict, L. P. Hubbard, Joseph E. Brush and George Sellick up to vote.

It was invariably the case in those days that a sufficient number of voters to fill the offices would not attend the meetings except upon personal solicitation, and Billy and I did most of the roping in. My part was to carry the lantern. He had an odd but very polite way of touching his hat and saying, "Please, sir, there are only four at the meeting and it takes eight to fill the offices. Won't you come up and vote for somebody, and somebody will vote for you?"

Such an appeal was irresistible and we elected the full Board. I can remember no other moderator in that building on election days except Amos M. Brush.

In those times there was not such a system of registration and such a poll list as are now employed. Of course, the Town Clerk's record showed who were voters and when they became voters. Both political parties were represented at the polls and there was always a record of the number of votes deposited.

Mr. Brush, the moderator, stood behind the ballot box and as the voter deposited his ballot Mr. Brush would poke it down among the others with his lead pencil. On one occasion a voter, whose political belief was opposed to that of the moderator, charged the latter with not depositing his ballot in the box. "Stop the voting," said Mr. Brush, "unlock the box and count the ballots," which was quickly done, and the disgruntled voter was satisfied that his ballot was among the others and not upon the floor, as he had charged.

In the old days when the town building on Greenwich Avenue was filled with tenants, a local wit dubbed it "Lincoln's Inn," and a young man who then resided here but who subsequently became a grave and learned professor in a great American University wrote the following lines which were pub-

THE OLD TOWN HALL

lished in the *Stamford Herald*. The first and last verses only are quoted:

> Oh, I wish I lived in Lincoln's Inn
> Where the signs are made of gilt and tin;
> With my feet in a chair I'd sit and grin,
> It's the way they do in Lincoln's Inn.
>
> .   .   .   .
>
> Then at night when the darkness is complete,
> When the faithful watchman treads his beat,
> And his boots resound in the silent street,
> Full many a spectre, weird, he sees,
> The ghosts of departed lawyers' fees
> And spirits pale of all degrees,
> Who perch in the dark; on the signs of tin—
> Oh, a rare old place is Lincoln's Inn.

CHAPTER XXI

L EWIS and Mason Streets are named after two prominent old-time families. One of the most interesting spots in the Borough, rife as it is with historic memories, is the northeast corner of Putnam Avenue and Lafayette Place, where the Rev. Dr. Lewis lived, and which was subsequently owned by his daughter, Mrs. Mary E. Mason, and his grandson, Theodore L. Mason, M.D.

Before the war of the Revolution this corner and many acres besides belonged to Henry Mead. He was the landlord of a Colonial tavern which stood near the junction of the main country road and the road to Sherwood's Bridge, now Glenville. Here he entertained, in such style as the times permitted, Gen. Putnam, Gen. Lafayette and other Revolutionary notables.

Times were hard in Greenwich after the close of the war and Henry Mead struggled along for a few years and then moved with his family to New York City. As far as is known, none of them returned.

He sold the old homestead or tavern in 1787 for three hundred and twenty pounds. The land, bounded northerly by the highway and what is now the Lenox House property and westerly by the road to Piping Point, now Greenwich Avenue, was purchased from Amos Mead and Henry Mead, respectively.

Lewis Street divides the southerly tract and was very appropriately named after Dr. Lewis.

He was a man of note throughout New England. He was graduated from Yale College in the class of 1765, and entered the ministry of the Congregational Church. His long and laborious professional life was largely passed in the pastorate of the Second Congregational Society in this town, which position he assumed in 1786 and occupied for thirty-three years. In 1792 Yale College conferred on him the degree of Doctor of Divinity, and from 1816 to 1818 he was a member of the Corporation, and in 1816 was made a Fellow of the College. Upon acquiring the property he at once proceeded to remove the Henry Mead house, and as the church then had no parsonage, he built a fine Colonial mansion about seventy-five feet back from the corner.

The old fig tree, still there, was planted by him and it grew very near the south end of the house. It was a beautiful house in all its proportions and in the look of hospitality which always pervaded it. It was built in the summer of 1786, but was not an old-fashioned sweep-back, because the Colonies had become independent, and the necessity for a one-story house, which is said to have been exempt from taxation by the Crown, no longer existed.

I have had many interesting conversations with the

late Col. Thomas A. Mead, Solomon S. Mead, D. Smith Mead and Isaac L. Mead concerning this old mansion. There was no conflict among them as to the location and appearance of the house. As the fig tree grew near the south end, it is easy to locate it. The house faced the west, and from the front door, over which was an old-time porch with a graceful trellis, a walk between rows of box-wood lead to Lafayette Place.

It was considered a grand house and its owner was looked up to by old and young as a wise and good man. It was his home for thirty-three years, and during that period it was the center of social and religious activities. "He was kind and affectionate in his social relations, and for piety and learning eminently distinguished," according to his epitaph. It is easy to believe he wielded a powerful influence for good in the community.

Dr. Lewis died August 27, 1840, at the age of ninety-five, leaving six children and a considerable estate.

Here, also, on November 20, 1821, died, at the early age of twenty-four, Miss Elizabeth Stillson of Bethlehem, Conn., a member of the family of Dr. Lewis, for whom the Stillson Benevolent Society of the Second Congregational Church was named.

The children who survived Dr. Lewis were Zachariah; Isaac, who succeeded his father as pastor of the church; Mrs. Platt Buffett of Stanwich; Mrs. Mary E. Mason, widow of David Mason; Roswell W., and

THE LEWIS AND MASON FAMILIES

Sarah. Mrs. Hannah Lewis, the mother of these children, died in April, 1829.

On the 10th of December, 1846, all the Lewis property was conveyed to Mary E. Mason and Sarah Lewis, and until 1850 they were inmates of the old mansion. Later they moved to the new house which was built in that year and is still standing. Mary E. Mason was the mother of Dr. Theodore L. Mason, for whom Mason Street, opened in 1881, was appropriately named.

MISS SARAH LEWIS
1784–1860

Miss Sarah Lewis was very active in the church that for so many years had been under the pastorate of her father and brother. She organized the Sunday School, and was its first superintendent. Her portrait hangs upon the wall in the Sunday School room.

In 1801 David Mason, Esq., married Mary Elizabeth Lewis, daughter of the Rev. Dr. Lewis, at the old homestead. He was a lawyer of ability and as an advocate had special influence. He was engaged in practice in Cooperstown, N. Y., with Mr. William Cooper, an elder brother of James Fenimore Cooper.

His cousin was Jeremiah Mason of Boston, who in his day often crossed swords with Daniel Webster in the courts of Massachusetts and New Hampshire.

[247]

David Mason was the father of three children, of whom Theodore L. Mason was the eldest. At his death his widow and children removed to Dr. Lewis' residence in Greenwich, where Theodore's youth and early manhood were spent. Under the direction of various teachers, and notably in the private school of his uncle, the Rev. Platt Buffett of Stanwich, he received a thorough training in English and the

DR. DARIUS MEAD
In 1860
1788–1864

classics. Later he became a medical student under the direction of Dr. Darius Mead, who lived on the top of Putnam Hill where Edwin H. Baker's house now stands. Dr. Mead gave the young men who studied under him clinical instruction at the bedside of the sick, as well as instruction in the proper text books.

Subsequently young Dr. Mason was graduated from the College of Physicians and Surgeons in New York and practiced a few months in Greenwich. He then went to Wilton, Conn., and later to New York City, removing from there to Brooklyn, N. Y., in 1834, where he remained in the active practice of his profession until his death February 12, 1882. He frequently visited Greenwich and during his life

[248]

was well known in this town. After his death the land on both sides of Mason and Lewis Streets as well as that along Greenwich Avenue was sold.

CHAPTER XXII

THE OLD BLACK WALNUT TREE

THE great black walnut tree that stands on Mrs. George E. Nichols' front lawn on Maple Avenue is said to be the largest in the State. It is certainly a very old tree and was a seedling long before the Revolution. It must have been planted very early in the eighteenth century and it is not improbable that the Rev. Abraham Todd, a minister who served the Second Congregational Church for forty years, planted it with his own hands. At that time and until 1833 the church owned no parsonage, but in addition to his salary the minister was given the use of the "parsonage lands."

Mr. Todd was graduated from Yale in 1727 and came to Greenwich five years later. For those days his salary was princely. He received a "settlement" of one thousand dollars, the use of the parsonage lands and five hundred dollars per annum, besides firewood, and after three years an additional one hundred and fifty dollars per annum.

As Mr. Todd on the 29th of May, 1733, purchased for eleven hundred dollars twelve acres of land of Theophilus Peck, with his homestead, we may assume that the "settlement" money above referred to

THE OLD BLACK WALNUT TREE

was thus invested and here was established the parsonage.

These twelve acres were identical with the land now extending from Patterson Avenue south to property of Edward Brush and west beyond Maher

SACKETT HOMESTEAD

Built 1779. Subsequently the homes of James W. Dominick and John Sniffen. Remodeled 1850. The old tree does not appear in the photograph

Avenue. In this tract stood for many years the John Sniffin house. When Mr. Todd bought the land it was bounded on the east by North Street, the name by which Maple Avenue was known until long after the adoption of a Borough government in 1854.

The house occupied by Mr. Todd until his death

in 1773 stood well back from the road, in what was subsequently called the old orchard. Mr. Alvan Mead, who died at an advanced age in 1881, was able to locate the house by tradition and to describe it as an old-fashioned sweep-back, facing the south.

Mr. Todd left seven children. Five years after his death they sold, for twenty-three hundred and fifty dollars, the place occupied by the family for more than forty years. Nehemiah Mead, Jr., was the purchaser and it may not be uninteresting to copy the description of the property as it appears in his deed. He purchased from the Todd heirs "Fourteen acres, "be it more or less, with a dwelling house and barn "thereon, northward of the Country road (meaning "what is now Putnam Avenue) it being that house "and land whereon our honored father, Rev. Abra-"ham Todd, deceased, lately lived. Bounded East-"erly by North Street, Northerly by land of "Humphrey Denton, Westerly by land of Justus "Sackett in part and partly by land of Isaac Holmes, "Jr., and Southerly by land of Justus Sackett."

Mr. Mead held it for only nine months when, on December 4, 1778, he sold it for one pound more than he paid to Justus Sackett.

It was Mr. Sackett who built the original John Sniffin homestead under the shade of the old black walnut tree and it was probably built immediately after he came into possession, in the Summer of 1779. Here he lived until January 15, 1827, when he died at the age of eighty-seven years.

THE OLD BLACK WALNUT TREE

In passing it may not be amiss to quote from Mr. Sackett's will in which he speaks of the "Todd lots," referring to the location near the old orchard, the former home of Rev. Abraham Todd. This spot is not far from the place occupied by the recently removed and remodeled "Sniffen homestead" on Patterson Avenue belonging to William H. Hoggson. To his son he gives his black boy "Charles" and the ancestral tall clock, showing that slavery was extant in Connecticut as late as 1815, when the will was dated, and that the tall clock was then valued more than by later generations.

Anna Sackett, the widow, continued to reside in the homestead in the enjoyment of her dower until February 15, 1837, when she died at the age of ninety-six years. Justus Sackett, Jr., was the next owner of the property. He appears to have been somewhat of a trader in real estate, for in 1832 he acquired contiguous property extending north and west as far as Sanford Mead's and south to Augustus Lyon's, later known as the Perry land and now belonging to William G. and Percy A. Rockefeller. He did not hesitate to borrow money and give mortgages, a somewhat unusual proceeding in those days. But on March 19, 1846, he seems to have been willing to abdicate in favor of his son, William H. Sackett, to whom he gave a deed of more than fifty acres, reserving to himself a life estate.

William H. Sackett continued to reside in the old homestead under the famous tree until 1851 when he sold the property to Justus Ralph Sackett, who held it until October 1, 1852, when he sold and conveyed it to James W. Dominick. And now we get down to the memory of many Greenwich people.

James W. Dominick and his brother, William, who resided on Putnam Avenue in the house now owned by Mrs. Susan C. Talbot, were two of the early Greenwich commuters. They each possessed a family of likely boys, who have sustained their early reputations and are now men, well known in financial circles being honored and respected by all. George F. Dominick and his son of the same name are both residents, but James W. Dominick's sons have never lived here.

Mr. James W. Dominick was rated a rich man and he belonged to a lineage of culture and refinement. Therefore the old Sackett homestead built in 1779 was not to his liking. It is true it possessed some attractive features, both within and without. The wide fireplace, the quaint mantel cupboards, the long shingles and the colonial roof with its diminutive dormers were artistic, but more room was needed and hence, more than fifty years ago, the remodeling was accomplished. Until it was moved in 1906 to make room for the new Nichols house it remained unchanged. It went to John Sniffen May 19, 1864, and continued in his possession until his death January 31, 1888. It was subsequently sold by the widow and heirs.

THE OLD BLACK WALNUT TREE

The Sackett boys, the Dominick boys and the Sniffen boys all had a happy home under the old black walnut tree which may continue to grow for centuries to come.

CHAPTER XXIII

AMONG the cherished articles of personal property found among the effects of the late Solomon Mead and now owned by his nephew, Elbert A. Silleck, is a map of "Rocky Neck Point." Exactly given, the title of the map is as follows: "Map "of eleven acres of land lying on Rocky Neck Point, "Greenwich steamboat landing, laid out into build- "ing lots 50 feet front on the road, unless otherwise "expressed upon the map and extending to the water. "Surveyed October, 1836, and plotted from a scale of "132 feet to one inch by Wm. H. Holly, N. Currier "Lith., Cor. Nassau and Spruce Streets, N. Y."

The map shows Indian Harbor Point, Field Point and an island then called Great Island, but now Round Island. It also shows the depth of water at the steamboat landing to be six feet at low tide, and it indicates the course of a steamboat to Stamford and Sawpits. The latter place now has the more dignified name of Port Chester. At the foot of the map is written in ink, "the above lots to be sold on the 23d of March, 1837." This is suggestive of a vendue, as an auction in those days was called. There were fifty-eight lots and one acre on the extreme point was reserved.

From the fact that this map was lithographed by the firm afterwards so well known as Currier & Ives, it is clear that the public vendue must have been extensively advertised.

At that time New York City was a day's journey away and was reached usually by market sloop and sometimes by team down the stage road.

Greenwich was then sparsely settled, devoted to agriculture exclusively, and possessed of considerable wealth. The land in question was wild, filled with rocks, and seamed with ledges overshadowed by enormous trees. The eleven acres included all the land south of the north line of the property of William H. Teed.

It appears from the records that as early as 1725, all the land from Grigg Street south to the end of the point and east as far as the Held House was called "Rockie Necke." It was common land, as wild as the Adirondack forest. About that time it was apportioned off by the town to the different taxpayers, who were called "Proprietors," in proportion to their respective assessment lists. Under the apportionment and by a few subsequent conveyances all of "Rockie Necke" went into the possession of two brothers, Daniel Smith and John Smith.

Through the marriage of a daughter of Daniel Smith much of this property went to Daniel Smith Mead, the grandfather of Oliver D. Mead.

When the Rocky Neck Co. was formed Daniel Smith Mead was deceased and the company bought the land of his heirs. This purchase represented the first effort of land speculators in Greenwich.

I often talked with those interested in the venture and I recall very distinctly the details of the transaction as they were given to me and as they are found in the public records. It was a wild and rocky stretch with nothing but a cart path over the line of the present highway.

No attempt had been made to cultivate any part of it. Many of the primeval forest trees were still standing—great oaks that had stretched their limbs across the Indian paths of a century earlier. There were bowlders of enormous size covered with a wealth of moss, and resting in beds of lichens and ferns that grew with rank luxuriance about their base. One larger and more rustic than all the others was shaped like a great chair, filled with moss and backed with cedars over which the woodbine trailed in graceful profusion. It was well named the "Indian Chief's Throne." To cut such a piece of land as that into fifty-eight building lots seemed a wild and chimerical scheme.

But as I read the list of stockholders of the Rocky Neck Co. I find them all men of nerve and character, as far as I knew them, and I have a personal knowledge of all but three. These were John D. Spader, who held three shares, Benjamin Andrews, two shares and Thomas Simons four shares. Mr. Spader was the man who subsequently married a daughter of Silas Davis and the other two were probably residents of New York.

The other stockholders were Silas Davis, one share; Augustus Lyon, five shares; William A. Husted, two shares; Jonathan A. Close, three shares; Walter Davis, one share; Alvan Mead, one share; Solomon Mead, three shares; Daniel S. Mead, one share; Zaccheus Mead, Jr., two shares; Husted Hobby, two shares; Abraham B. Davis, three shares; and Thomas A. Mead, two shares. Each share had a par value of one hundred dollars.

Silas Davis appears to have been the leader of the enterprise, as he held what was termed a refusal of the property for $3500. At the present time it would be called a thirty-day option, except that Mr. Davis had nothing in writing. But perhaps he was merely carrying out the instructions of such men as Solomon Mead and Thomas A. Mead in securing the option. At that time Solomon Mead was only twenty-eight years old and as he lived here all his life and died at the age of ninety, possessed of more than a million of dollars, it is fair to assume that this apparently crazy investment was advised and perhaps urged by him. Although he thought the price too high, he finally approved the scheme, put up his three hundred dollars and carefully preserved the map, possibly as a reminder that in this enterprise he made some of his first dollars.

The company was formed under the joint stock laws, and the articles of the association which appear in the land records were evidently prepared by a lawyer.

OTHER DAYS IN GREENWICH

The purpose of the association was to acquire the land and to build a store house or store houses, and a wharf in order that passengers and freight to Stamford, New York and other points could be transported. This was clearly a bid to steamboats and sailing vessels to call for passengers and produce, but no suggestion was made that the company should engage in the transportation business.

The corporation was, however, to be a close one and a special provision was made whereby any stock seeking a purchaser must be offered to the other stockholders. This was too good a thing to afford even a taste to outsiders.

The first meeting was called for September 14, 1836, at seven o'clock in the evening at the inn of Augustus Lyon. The name of that inn, which was one of the stage stops on the mail route between New York and Boston, was "The Mansion House," since known as the Lenox House. Here all the incorporators gathered and evidently without any lawyer, because all they did was to sign the articles of incorporation. There appears to have been no election of officers or directors. However, we can imagine what a jolly time these young men had in the front room of the inn that September night. They all put up their money, and in due time the land was conveyed and in the following month "Bill Hen" Holly, of Stamford, as everybody called him, made the survey and map.

The following Spring sales began to be made, but

they were not very active and many times the owners were almost discouraged.

It is not unreasonable to suppose that most of the buyers were discouraged too, for Captain Abraham Brinckerhoff, who bought one of the lots from the map, discovered when he made his way in between

RESERVED LOT IN 1876 SHOWING EPHRAIM READ HOME-STEAD IN FOREGROUND AND THE MARBLE HOUSE BEYOND

the rocks and trees, that in order to reach his lot he would have to buy two more.

The map shows one acre reserved on the extreme point. This was afterwards known as the Ephriam Read property and includes the Indian Harbor yacht club house and grounds and the cottage sites on the east side of the road, built by Charles T. Wills, now owned by the Indian Harbor yacht club. The incorporators all agreed that the reservation should be made, but no two of them thought alike as to the purpose of the reservation. One wanted it for a com-

[261]

mon cow pasture, after the trees were removed, for the use of those who might buy and build on the lots. Another suggested that such a dense forest would supply sufficient firewood for all who might buy lots. Another urged the erection of a cider mill. William A. Husted thought that the lumber could be shipped to New York at a large profit and the cleared ground used for an apple orchard. Col. Mead [who, by the way, had no such title then, but was just Thomas] and Solomon Mead thought that as the reservation had been made, there was no immediate necessity of passing upon the question of its disposition. They thought that would take care of itself, and indeed it did.

Four of the company built potato cellars where the Silleck House now stands. They were built with openings at either end, like the one on Round Island, which bears the date, 1827. These cellars belonged to Solomon Mead, Thomas A. Mead and Zaccheus Mead, Jr., but it is uncertain who owned the fourth one. The Silleck House was erected over these very cellars in 1838, just one year after they were built.

This building, a small affair, owned by Jared Mead, proved to be unsuccessful. Situated near the shore with a dense forest on three sides, it was an ideal spot for a quiet summer retreat. The trouble with the "White House," as Mr. Mead called it, was due to the fact that table supplies were difficult to obtain. At that time there was no market in Greenwich. To supply the table with meat it was Jared

Mead's custom to purchase lambs and calves of the farmers and butcher them on the premises. Vegetables were secured at the market sloops. Butter was difficult to buy as the farmers preferred to send it to New York. The cows were pastured on Field Point, assuring a good supply of milk and cream. The water was brought from one of the Field Point springs, there being no well near the hotel. Apples were free to anyone who would gather them.

Mr. Mead had a good class of boarders at what was then thought to be remunerative prices, but he found it quite a struggle to maintain a satisfactory table. His fried fish, broiled lobsters, succulent oysters and scallops were considered most palatable, but there always came a time when the appetite demanded fresh meat.

In the spring of 1849, when the railroad was just six months old, he sold out to Mrs. Fanny Runyan and Mrs. Mary Dennis. These ladies, although they were joint owners of the real estate, were partners in business only one summer. On the 9th of February, 1850, Mrs. Dennis sold out to Thomas Funston. His wife was Mrs. Runyan's sister and Mrs. Elbert A. Silleck is his granddaughter.

In the winter of 1854-5 upon the death of Mrs. Funston, Mr. Funston sold his interest to Thaddeus Silleck, although he did not take title till May 25 of the latter year.

The Silleck House is the oldest hotel on either shore of the Sound from Sands' Point to Stonington.

OTHER DAYS IN GREENWICH

These details have been carefully gathered for the reason that it has many times been erroneously stated that Thaddeus Silleck was the founder of the hotel bearing his name since 1876.

Mrs. Runyan died at Rocky Neck Jan. 26, 1913, aged 98. From her I obtained many interesting facts about the White House long before the war. Imagine board at $2.50 per week! And yet she and Mr.

JOHN G. WELLSTOOD
1813–1893
Father of Town Clerk Wellstood

Silleck had many serious conferences that first year of their partnership over the advisability of increasing the rate a single dollar. But when it was done, to their great surprise, nobody objected and they found it just as easy to collect the $3.50 as the old rate.

The old registers show the class of boarders was exceptionally good. Among them were Prof. King of Columbia College, W. B. Taylor, the New York postmaster, Robert M. Bruce, Horace Greeley, Charles A. Whitney, John G. Wellstood, Charles G. Cornell, Peter Asten, Archibald Parks, John Hoey, afterwards President of the Adams Express Co., and his talented wife, for many years the leading lady at Wallack's.

Years ago there was a fascination about Greenwich

that to some extent has disappeared. The place was rather inaccessible, the roads were poor, there were no sidewalks or modern conveniences of any kind, but there was the beautiful Sound, serene skies, the broad fields, with no barbed wire fences or trespass signs, so that all the blessings seemed to be individual in which one's ownership was perfect.

This is probably what made Greenwich so popular when once established as a place of quiet enjoyment. The children and the grandchildren of many of those early boarders are still patronizing the Silleck House.

The old land company has been well-nigh side-tracked. Let us see how it finished. The amount invested had been small but the stockholders sighed for dividends, and some were so disappointed that they sold out to the others at a loss. But the reserved acre on the point saved the day to those who held on and about 1850 all the land had been sold at constantly increasing prices. When the final settlement was made there was distributed to the survivors a net profit of a substantial amount.

Before Solomon Mead died, that reserved acre had been sold for about fifty thousand dollars. How much Solomon Mead made out of his first venture is unknown, but he was one of the survivors and he always said he was satisfied with the result.

When I look at the map that he folded away so many years ago, I am inclined to believe that he regarded the Rocky Neck Land Co. as the corner stone of his great fortune.

CHAPTER XXIV

RAILROADS IN THE EARLY DAYS

EARLY in the nineteenth century there was considerable activity in our General Assembly, in granting charters to railroads. The turnpikes and canals of the preceding century had proved remunerative and it was reasoned that railroads as means of transportation would be still more profitable.

In 1832 the Norwich & Worcester was incorporated, followed in 1836 by the Housatonic; the New York & New Haven in 1844; the Naugatuck in 1845, and the New Haven & Northampton in 1846.

I am not aware when these roads were constructed but the New Haven R. R. sent its first train through Greenwich on Christmas day, 1848. Among the passengers from New York was William Henry Mead and he is the last survivor of the Greenwich people who were on that train. He was also on the first trolley car that came up Greenwich Avenue, August 17, 1901.

It has been said that the first construction of the New Haven railroad was quite a crude affair. But in 1859 it was double-tracked and had in a great measure recovered from the financial difficulties into which its first president, Robert Schuyler of New York, had plunged it.

RAILROADS IN THE EARLY DAYS

In the early days a stockholder, and there were many in Greenwich, was never willing to admit that he owned a share. Owing to what were termed the "Schuyler frauds" and also to great losses occasioned by the Norwalk disaster which occurred May 6, 1853, when a train ran into an open draw and killed fifty passengers, the stock had very little value. At that time Justin R. Buckley of New York was president

LOCOMOTIVE NO. 27
N. Y. & N. H. R. R.

and among the directors were Capt. William L. Lyon of Greenwich and J. W. Leeds of Stamford.

Capt. Lyon owned and occupied what is now known as the John Voorhis homestead on Putnam Avenue, with extensive gardens and lawns extending along Greenwich Avenue as far south as the garage of Allen Brothers. He was the grandfather of Luke Vincent Lockwood.

James H. Hoyt of Stamford was Superintendent and he possessed greater power and influence in the management of the road than the president, who was little known in Connecticut. Superintendent Hoyt was the father of George H. Hoyt, who began his business career as ticket agent in the Stamford station and at the time of his death had, for many years, been president of the Stamford Savings Bank.

The rails were light, rarely meeting at the ends, being plugged with a block of wood. The rails rested

MOSES CRISTY
1817–1884

on what were called "chairs" and were not fastened so as to make a practically continuous rail as at present. To travel on such a railroad required considerable fortitude as well as patience.

Greenwich had seven trains each way in 1859 and no Sunday trains. There were five trains to New York in the morning, namely the 5.20, 6.36, 7.21, 8.37 and 11.36. The 7.21 was the popular morning train, used by the commuters, of whom there were a very limited number. Of these I recall Robert M. Bruce, John G. Wellstood, Charles A. Whitney, Moses Christy, Luther Prescott Hubbard and Henry M. Benedict.

From New York the first train left Twenty-seventh Street at 7 A. M. The cars were drawn up Fourth Avenue—four horses to each car—to 32nd Street [a little later to 42nd Street] where a wood burning engine was attached. Think of such a thing happening now in front of the new Vanderbilt Hotel!

The first stop was at Williamsbridge at 7.37. This was originally the northern terminus of the Harlem railroad, the first railroad built out of New York, and on the north side of the track may still be seen the remains of the foundation of the old turntable.

The stations following were Mt. Vernon, New Rochelle, Mamaroneck, Rye and Port Chester, reaching Greenwich at 8.21. There were no such stations as Columbus Ave., 125th St., Pelham, Larchmont or Harrison. There was at that time no South Norwalk, but at the Norwalk station a horse car line ran to the Borough of Norwalk.

The time table of that year, a bit of yellow paper, printed on both sides and only six by ten inches in size, is among my possessions. The difference between that modest little affair and the through time table of to-day, with its sixty-two pages, represents the difference in the importance of the road then and at the present time.

This was before the days of consolidations and the inconveniences of transportation of half a century ago have been eliminated by the union of corporations.

We take a parlor car at New York, and in five hours, having had all the comforts of a delightful journey, step out at the South Station in Boston. But on this little yellow time table there is no assurance that the Boston express—there were two daily—

would ever carry you beyond New Haven. That was the end of the line and upon arrival you were turned over to another road. If the trains made good connections you might expect to reach Boston in seven hours, including ten minute stops for refreshments, at such points as Hartford, Springfield and Worcester. You were in charge of a new set of trainmen, without uniforms, and you jogged on over a rough roadbed, dodging hot cinders from the engine and swaying back and forth in the narrow rigid seats.

There existed scarcely a community of interest between the New Haven road, seventy-two miles long, and the other roads of the State. The first train out of New York left at 7 A. M. and passengers for the Danbury & Norwalk R. R. were told to take that train and change cars at Norwalk. The same remark was made of the Housatonic, the Naugatuck and New London R. R. Companies. Each was an independent concern, never waiting beyond its time of departure. The New Haven road simply suggested, but not in words, "we will take you where you can find another railroad and you take your chances."

But the road was making money and paying ten per cent dividends, with a good surplus in the treasury. Indeed the law makes it compulsory to pay to the State all railroad earnings in excess of ten per cent unless the same is required for equipment or roadbed. It is needless to say that the State has never received a dividend. There were enough op-

Upper right hand corner shows ORIGINAL STATION of the NEW HAVEN RAILROAD IN 1848 located on Center Street. Left hand picture represents 27th STREET DEPOT OF THE NEW HAVEN and 26th STREET DEPOT OF THE HARLEM RAILROAD. These were in use until 1871. Lower corner shows CHANGE FROM HORSES TO LOCOMOTIVES AT 32nd STREET.

portunities to make improvements and one of these was in new locomotives.

When No. 27 came out the directors gave Currier & Ives of New York a commission to make lithograph prints, in colors, of the engine and they were given away to friends of the road. It was a light

GREENWICH R. R. STATION 1859

affair, with a great bulging smoke stack, the driving wheels painted a gay red, but half the weight of an ordinary yard engine of the present day.

In the spring of 1868 two parlor cars were put on the Boston express trains. These it was believed would add materially to the comfort of the traveler. These cars were of the English Coach model, divided into compartments with a door from each opening onto the running board. They were called "New York" and "Boston" and left each city about eight o'clock. They were supplied by the Wagner Parlor Car Co. They were never popular and the following year one was destroyed in a train shed fire and the other was withdrawn.

The club car was unknown in those days but certain commuters who desired to play cards occupied their own camp chairs in the baggage car. These chairs were in charge of the baggage master, who had little else to do, and his compensation was a generous Christmas collection. This was the origin of the present club car service.

The location of the Greenwich station in 1859 was about seventy feet north of the present site but the building now in use is the same, enlarged and improved, when the four tracks were laid in 1893.

It was a quiet spot, where that old station stood fifty years ago. Henry Sackett's great farm barn across the road, south of where the Daly building now stands, gave forth an aroma of the country as the passengers left the train and walked past it on a lane twelve feet wide to Greenwich Avenue. There was always one hack in attendance, owned and operated by William Elliott. He was a man of various responsibilities, for besides being the hackman he was the ticket agent, baggage master and hotel proprietor. He was just such a bustling type of thin, sinewy man as one finds to-day occupying similar positions, at remote little stations in Maine and New Hampshire.

In those days there was no telegraph station and

WILLIAM H. WALLACE
At age of 16

it was years afterwards before the Adams Express Co. took any notice of Greenwich.

It was Mr. Elliott's custom to sit on the station platform during the long summer days, fighting flies and dozing away the time between trains, while the boys would sneak up behind him and tickle his ears with a timothy head. When they tired of this, they would go down under the stone arch, after which the street has since been named, and, hurrying along the dusty road in their haste to get into the water at

CHARLES H. WRIGHT
Age of 24
1834–1878

the head of the creek, shed their clothing, one piece after another, until there was scarcely a pause before they were nude and immersed.

But the boys' fun was considerably curtailed after Mr. Elliott employed William H. Wallace as an assistant. Although "Billy" Wallace was then only sixteen years old he felt the responsibilities of his position and the boys had to stop fooling around the station, although it was several years before the swimming hole was abandoned.

There wasn't much for young Wallace to do but paint the chairs and scrub the floors, but he made the old station such a model one that it attracted the attention of the officials. His reputation for cleanliness must have been well established among the school children, for I know that the following incident actually occurred: One day Charles H. Wright, the

[276]

principal of the public school, was walking along the track with a favorite scholar. The summer sun was just sinking in the west as the man and boy looked ahead at the glittering rails and exclaimed "How beautiful!" At their feet the iron was dull and tarnished but where the sunlight struck them, in front of the station and down at the Field Point crossing, the rails shone like burnished silver.

WILLIAM H. WALLACE
As Asst. Supt. N. Y., N. H. & H. R. R.

"It is the finger of God in the sunshine, my boy, that turns this homely iron to those threads of silver," said the teacher. The boy replied, "Oh, no. Billy Wallace has been scouring 'em."

However, Mr. Wallace secured the confidence of the officials and became the first baggage master at the station. Then he succeeded Mr. Elliott as ticket agent and from freight conductor to conductor of one of the finest through trains, he finally became assistant superintendent, which position he held for many years, with an office at New Haven. He died at his home on Milbank Avenue April 5, 1906.

In those days there were no through freight trains; one local that ran down in the forenoon and back at night. Conductor Jones was in charge with old engine No. 10. He knew everybody on the line and after his freight was loaded he was sometimes reluctant to leave till an especially good story was told.

The milk train down at 10.30 at night was sometimes used by passengers who occupied the caboose.

The conductors and brakemen were not compelled to wear a uniform, the only mark of their official position being a piece of metal, fastened to the front of the cap marked "Conductor" or "Brakeman." But the conductor then had all the responsibility of running his train, while now the trains are controlled by the tower men. They were often the recipients of presents from commuters in the form of gold watches and lanterns of rich cut glass, bearing the name of the official.

The cars were low, and covered with a flat roof, without ventilators, with very small windows and lighted by four coach lamps containing coal oil. This absence of light required the conductor to have a lantern on his arm while punching and collecting tickets and reading by the passengers was impossible. At each end of the car was a long wood stove, by the side of which was a wood box, usually filled with white birch. The brakeman attended to the fire and "broke" the train at the call of the engineer by two sharp whistles.

Every train carried a "water boy" whose duty it was to go through the train occasionally and supply the passengers with water carried in a tin receptacle resembling a watering pot, without the rose, and surrounded by half a dozen glasses in tin brackets.

RAILROADS IN THE EARLY DAYS

Many of the old time conductors rose from the humble post of water boy, entering the service at the age of fourteen.

It was certainly no easy task to travel and yet I recall one occasion when I rode with my father over the "Old Colony & Newport R. R.," such rolling stock as I have described was referred to as the "luxuries of travel" and so it was in comparison to the stage coach and canal which, as means of transportation, had been abandoned but comparatively few years.

LOOKING DOWN THE HARBOR 1859 FROM NEAR R. R. STATION

PRIOR to 1870 Riverside was unnamed and Sound Beach was Old Greenwich. A century earlier it was "Old Town." All that portion of the town now known as Sound Beach is historic ground. In 1640 it was called Monakawaye, that name gradually limiting itself to the point, which, a few years later, became Elizabeth Neck, which name it retained for many years. Later, it bore the name of Old Greenwich Point and J. Kennedy Tod calls it Innis Arden.

It received its first English name from Elizabeth Feaks, who, under the first Indian deed, became a part owner of that territory and with her husband, John Feaks, lived on the beautiful point. "Good Ma Feaks," as she was called, was a daughter of John Winthrop, who was Governor of Massachusetts with little intermission from 1630 until his death in 1649. She and her husband, with Capt. Daniel Patrick, Capt. John Underhill, Jeffre Ferris, and a few others, were the first settlers of Greenwich and they established themselves along the shore of the Sound.

Patrick and Underhill were fighting characters and gallantly shared with Capt. John Mason, another fighting man, the hardships and glories of the Pequot War in 1637. The other settlers were men of peace.

Feaks and Patrick came to Greenwich early in 1640. They were acting under the authority and in behalf of the Colony of New Haven and they at once opened negotiations with the Senawaye Indians for the purchase of land for a settlement. The red men, caring less for land than for coats and blankets, were quite willing to part with their ancient possessions, and on July 18, 1640, they formally executed to Feaks and Patrick a conveyance of a large tract including all of what is now Sound Beach. This deed was unrecorded for forty-five years, when it took its place in Vol. 1, page 1, of the Greenwich Land Records, where the copy now is, yellow and faded with age but perfectly legible, under a magnifying glass, and signed by old Amogorone, whose name is now associated with the Greenwich Fire Department.

In the early sixties there was nothing but open fields, beautiful trees, along the highways and a magnificent view at Sound Beach. Of course it had farmers and they were prosperous, because the soil was wonderfully productive—the place often being called the garden spot of Greenwich. The soil is black, free from ledge or bowlder and well adapted to the cultivation of celery, strawberries and asparagus. When it was out of season on the farm there was an oyster boat in the cove near by, for the Sound Beach farmer plowed the sea as well as the land.

The old Ferris homestead, still standing, was at the

entrance gate of the Sound shore, where scallops in large quantities were caught after the first of October. During the warm summer days after the hay had been gathered and the potatoes hoed for the last time, the farmers from Greenwich and Stamford, and some

even from Bedford, made it a point to give their families an outing on the broad beach or they would camp out for a week or two under the great oaks that grow on the point.

Riverside had no railroad station until about 1870. Both the station and the post office were established through the

LUKE A. LOCKWOOD
1833–1905

efforts of Jeremiah W. Atwater and Luke A. Lockwood. Mr. Atwater and his family came to Greenwich from Brooklyn and bought a house and lot of Titus Mead on February 27, 1865. The place was located on the west side of North Street and is now owned by William F. H. Lockwood. Mr. Atwater was a commuter on the railroad, having a real estate office in New York. Some three or four years afterwards he moved to what is now Riverside and began the active development of that part of the town. He bought large tracts at what were considered large prices but what he sold brought him a good profit. He also engaged in house con-

[282]

struction, building some of the best houses in Riverside and thus improving his land was better able to
dispose of it.

He was very optimistic and although the hard

AMASA A. MARKS
1825–1905

times of 1873 and the years that preceded the re-
sumption of specie payments made his schemes of
development more difficult, he never lost courage but
was always confident that in the end he would "come
in a sure winner," as, in fact, he did.

Luke A. Lockwood, a New York lawyer who lived
at the old homestead and died November 20, 1905, in

[283]

the house in which he was born, gave to Mr. Atwater hearty encouragement and thus were established the railroad station, a post office, and St. Paul's chapel, now an Episcopal Church independent of Christ Church, organized originally as a private corporation.

The growth and importance of Sound Beach may be largely attributed to the efforts of Amasa A. Marks. He was a New York manufacturer and business man, who came to Greenwich and, on January 12, 1872, bought of Charles Hendrie, Jr., about twenty-five acres of shore front land for $10,500. The price he paid for the land shows that he was a pioneer. The man who sold him the land was a native and the old homestead still stands, a beautiful example of an old-time mansion.

Mr. Charles Hendrie had a brother, J. W. Hendrie, who is well remembered by his neighbors at Sound Beach. He was a graduate of Yale College, a member of the famous class of 1851, and upon receiving his degree he embarked for California. In the city of San Francisco, where he was early a large land-owner, he became rich from the profits of the gold mines. The law school building at Yale, known as Hendrie Hall, was his gift.

Mr. Marks and Mr. Hendrie, who in those early days spent a few months each year at the old home-stead, coöperated as far as possible in the improvement of the roads, the construction of a new school building and in many other ways made their influence felt in the community. Mr. Marks left a son, William L. Marks, who is still a resident of Sound Beach, being the public spirited owner of Laddin's Rock Farm. George E. Marks, another son, who in his younger days was a civil engineer in town, is now a resident of New York City.

The advent of the railroad in 1848 led many of the old residents to believe that a station would be located in that neighborhood. Gilbert Marshall resided in the house still standing nearly opposite the present Sound Beach station. He owned considerable land in that vicinity and it was his desire to have a station at that point.

It is difficult to imagine for whose accommodation it was required, but Mr. Marshall was determined to get the station and he got it—on the map. In his deed of a part of the right of way he had his lawyer insert these words: "Said Company is to establish a "regular stopping place on said land and if said Com-"pany should fail to use it as a passenger depot for "three months at any one time after said road shall "have been completed between New Haven and New "York, then the said land shall revert to and become "the property of said Marshall."

The old man told me it was just as strong as Charles Hawley could write it and still the station remained a promise unfulfilled for thirty-one years and long after the old man had passed away. For years before his death I often saw him standing at the south door as the train rattled by looking as if he was still waiting and expecting the long deferred station.

CHAPTER XXVI

THE Greenwich Hospital on Milbank Avenue occupies land where formerly stood the Octagon House.

In the spring of 1859 this house stood alone in a wide territory of farm land. It had been built about two years. Mason Street, then called on a map in the Town Clerk's office "First Avenue," had not been opened and Milbank Avenue from Putnam Avenue to Davis Avenue was called Love Lane, sometimes Mill Lane. South of that it went by the name of Second Avenue.

Aaron Woolsey and Edwin Mead owned all that tract north of Elm Street bounded on the east by Milbank Avenue, on the west by Greenwich Avenue and extending north to the Mason property, now Lewis Street. This land was all very productive and from the Octagon House was an unbroken view, south and west across fields of timothy and grain.

Solomon S. Gansey built the house from plans claimed by him to be original. He said he expected to build a house of an entirely new and original style of architecture and the plan as first drawn showed one more story than was finally constructed. The third story for lack of funds was omitted and the cupola occupied its place.

Jacob T. Weed had an inn at the head of Greenwich Avenue, in those days, and among those who made the inn a place of rendezvous, particularly Sat-

THE OCTAGON HOUSE

urday nights, was the builder, Mr. Gansey. When Mr. Gansey showed the plans to Mr. Weed, the latter suggested that the house be built out of plumb, so as to resemble the leaning tower of Piza. Mr. Gansey told Mr. Weed that he didn't know what he meant, but that he had a suspicion that Mr. Weed was laughing at him.

However, the house construction went on with its

windows and doors on eight sides, till it was completed in the imperfect manner already described.

Brush Knapp was a native of Greenwich who, when he was a youth, had left the Round Hill farm for New York City. He became wealthy as a wholesale grocer and in 1850 retired, and purchased of William L. Lyon seven acres and a dwelling house on North Street, now the property of Cornelius Mead and lately occupied by George Guion.

On the second of April, 1859, he bought the Octagon house of George A. Palmer for $5,000, including one and one-half acres of land. The same month he bought of Aaron Woolsey of Bedford, N. Y., for $1,500 five acres adjoining his first purchase. At that time the opening of what is now Mason Street between Elm and the present Lewis Street was somewhat uncertain, as shown by Mr. Knapp's deed which reads as follows:

"In case the said Brush Knapp and adjoining "owners shall deside to keep it (First Avenue) per- "manently closed then each party shall own to the "center of said First Avenue, opposite the land owned "by him."

It was about ten years before this portion of Mason Street was opened and it held the name of First Avenue till 1881 when it was extended north to Putnam Avenue and the street, for its entire length, named Mason Street.

Mr. Knapp had been an active business man in

New York and for those days had amassed a fortune. He was pleased with the location and surroundings of the house, but he often stated that when the place was new to him he had to take his bearings with some care, lest in attempting to go out at the front door he emerged at the back door, so confusing was the construction of his eight sided house.

Mr. Knapp was a man of excellent judgment and was active in the management of Borough affairs, occupying the position of Burgess many terms. His keen business instinct enabled him as the B o r o u g h grew to sell off from time to time portions of

BRUSH KNAPP
At 75
1807–1895

his original purchase until he had gotten his money back several times over, and still retained his home with ample ground.

When Mason Street was opened from Elm Street to Lewis Street he built one of the first houses on the street, where his daughters, Amelia and Martha Knapp, lived for a number of years. The house is now owned by David K. Allen.

In 1885 Mr. Knapp sold the home to Mary Waring Mead and went to live in the Mason Street house, where his last days were spent.

CHAPTER XXVII

THE first house north of Cornelius Mead's on the road to Stanwich is the home of George P. Waterbury, known as Stonybrooke, and recently purchased by J. Howland Hunt. One hundred and seventy years ago this road was called the By-field Road. No one knows why it bore that name, but it is frequently mentioned in the early land records and may have referred to a road by a field, at a time when cleared ground was rare.

The house, which stands on a knoll beneath an ancient elm, looks out across a merry brook and down a road, curving between moss-covered stone walls. Beyond this road, with its graceful curves, is a broad stretch of meadow, called in the old deeds "the Hook land," and still farther away the trees of a dense forest meet the sky line.

The first settler on this spot, then common land, was Caleb Mead. He was born in 1693 and tradition has it that he was forty-one years old when he built the first house at Stonybrooke. It was on the exact spot where the present house stands. In 1750 at the age of fifty-six Caleb Mead died, leaving three sturdy sons, Caleb, Jeremiah and Titus.

Caleb, the father, left a will by which he gave all his land, divided and undivided, "lying in Greenwich Township, Fairfield County, Connecticut Colony, in New England," to be equally divided between his three sons, above mentioned. After his death the boys made division of the land by the exchange of quit claim deeds, and the homestead went to Jeremiah.

The following year, 1751, Jeremiah tore down the old house, and using some of the old frame, built the western half of the present house. The fireplaces in the kitchen and living-room and in the chambers above are suggestive of a time when they were the only means of cooking the food and warming the house. The eastern half of the house has been built within the last sixty years. That portion of the house first built, reveals massive oak beams, wrought iron nails and handmade latches and hinges that tell of house construction methods one hundred and fifty years ago.

It is probable that about this time the mill site on the property was first utilized.

While the dam was rebuilt in 1830 and bears that date, it is well known that the new dam gave place to one of more ancient construction and by some it has been claimed that Caleb Mead, the first settler, made use of the water power for a cider mill, traces of the foundations of which are still pointed out in the orchard south of the house. It is more likely, however, that the first use of the water power was for a saw mill. It is known that many of the earliest

THE OLD MILL AT STONYBROOKE
Inserts: Edmund Mead, first and second

houses in Greenwich were supplied with material sawed at that mill. Jeremiah Mead ran the mill and managed the farm during his life.

His son, Edmund Mead, taking up the work after his death, raised a family of twelve children. The lat-

LOWER FALLS, STONYBROOKE
Power for the churn and ice-cream freezer

ter consisted of six boys—James, Reuben, Allen, Alfred, Edmund and Irving, and six daughters, Laura, Eunice, Anna, Lydia, Emeline and Samantha. Upon the third son, Allen, the father of Dr. Beverly E. Mead, devolved early in life the management of the old mill. He measured the lumber and thereby learned to solve many a mathematical problem which

[295]

the school boys of those days could not master. He learned music when musical attainments were not looked upon with favor by the hard-working farmers, but Allen caught many a spare moment among the logs around the old mill to study the art of music as taught by Lowell Mason, a famous Boston teacher who had a class in Stamford.

Later, the farm descended to the son, Edmund, who ran the mill for many years and died at the old place May 9, 1893. He was the father of Irving Mead of Stanwich and of Mrs. John H. Banks of the Borough. It was less than thirty years ago that the mill wheel was stopped and the old mill was given over to the storage of plows and harrows. It was torn down about 1909.

The illustration shows how the old building rested against a great tree. But for that tree it would have fallen several years before it finally became unsafe. It was probably the last of its kind near the village and it was an interesting relic of the generations that have gone before.

SNAP SHOTS AT STONYBROOKE

CHAPTER XXVIII

IN an early chapter, reference has been made to the old Davis mill. It was a great disappointment to me that it had to be torn down, because I always loved the old mill. I caught eels under its great wheel before I was ten years old. I dove from the rocks into the pond, and swam with the tide through the race-way and as I grew older I fished for snappers from the window on the south side. I knew every mysterious nook and cranny in the old building.

But at last it grew so weak with age that it was no longer safe to allow it to stand. The upper part of the building was sound. Every timber and plank in it were hewn from the native forests and the marks of the adze were visible. Some of the oak was as hard as bone, but the sills and the lower floor timbers had for so many years felt the direct influence of the salt water that they were thoroughly decayed and there was great danger of a complete collapse.

The mill was built in 1705. At that time Church and State were closely united. Ecclesiastical property was town property. The meeting house, as the name indicates, was used for both religious and secular purposes. The minister was supported by the taxpayers, and the town meeting hired and discharged

[299]

as it saw fit. Rev. Joseph Morgan was the minister in that year and by a vote of the town, January 9, 1704, he was granted the privilege of building a mill on Cos Cob river.

The stream referred to as Cos Cob river was sometimes known as Brothers brook and later Davis' creek. Many have supposed that the river referred to is the creek at Cos Cob, but in this they are mistaken, as that was always called in the records the "Myanos river."

The grant to build the mill was accorded to Mr. Morgan with a view to aiding in his support, and as a convenience to the inhabitants who wanted their corn ground. But the mill was very profitable and it became a serious question with the deacons of the church whether Mr. Morgan was not devoting less time to the spiritual interests of his parish and more to the running of the mill than was best for those concerned.

The town had given to Mr. Morgan thirty acres of common land and a house lot where the village is now located, and the people thought he should be there most of the time, rather than at the mill.

There was, however, a difference of opinion as to whether Mr. Morgan was justified in his course and therefore at a town meeting held July 20, 1708, it was voted to leave the matter for decision to the ministers of the County, very much as such differences in these days would be settled.

Ebenezer Mead and Caleb Knapp were appointed

THE OLD MILL AT DAVIS LANDING 1868

a committee to lay the subject before the united ministry of Fairfield County and the result was adverse to Mr. Morgan. The ministers decided that Mr. Morgan ought to hire a competent miller, while its owner should attend to the spiritual wants of his parish.

The matter was decided with great promptness, but Mr. Morgan showed a reluctance to yield and on the 27th of August, 1708, the town voted that Mr. Morgan must obey or the committee should hire another minister by "ye last of September."

However, Mr. Morgan held out till the 17th of October, when he gave up the fight, stuck to his mill, and the committee secured another preacher.

The mill must have been a source of great profit, for after Mr. Morgan's death it was sold at auction for a large price, and what seems very singular to a man who had no interests here—to a genuine outsider by the name of Valentine. He lived in Oyster Bay, Long Island, then called "Nassau Island." He owned a trading sloop, that had frequently made a harbor in "Chimney Corner" and in that way Capt. Valentine knew of the value of the property and was present when it was offered for sale.

The Valentine family owned the old mill till 1761 when it was sold to Thomas Davis, who also came from Oyster bay. He ran the mill up to the time of the Revolutionary war. His two sons, Stephen and Elisha, ran it jointly during the war. Elisha Davis was a Tory and secretly ground grain for the British fleet lying in the Sound. Stephen Davis remained loyal and at the end of the war the State of Connecticut, being able to convict Elisha Davis of his offense, confiscated his property, which constituted the undivided half of the mill.

Afterwards, by an act of the General Assembly and in conformity with the treaty of peace with Great Britain, Stephen Davis bought back the share which had been taken from his brother and for many peaceful years thereafter the wheel went round with every tide for the convenience of the people and the profit of Stephen Davis.

For more than a century thereafter, the white-aproned miller that lifted the sacks of grain in at the old Dutch door and passed back the meal into the waiting ox cart, was a Davis.

Stephen Davis was laid at rest with his father on the hillside, in the woods just north of the railroad and was followed by his sons and his grandsons, all millers. There was Silas, Walter the "Commodore," Henry and last of all, Edward, who died in the winter of 1891.

He loved the old mill but he realized that its end had come and the day before the demolition began he went all through it in his half blindness. He passed his hands over the girders and the floor timbers and stroked the long shingles as though they were creatures of life and knew him and realized the parting hour. The warming pan, the old brass andirons and the ancient clock of his forefathers were all in

THE OLD MILL AT DAVIS LANDING

the mill, but were taken out with tender care and not
long since I saw the clock, now more than two hundred
years old, still ticking the time away in the shop of
Henry Schifferdecker.

Although the old mill is gone, all the surroundings
are much as they were fifty years ago. The winding
road with the wayside well, the picturesque walls,
the granite bowlders, moss-covered and overgrown
with stunted cedars and climbing vines, the bold and
wooded shores up and down the creek all lend a charm
to Davis Landing that the removal of the old mill
has not effaced.

CHAPTER XXIX

THE ANCIENT HIGHWAYS

THE highway commissioner, Leon H. Peck, says there are about one hundred and seventy-five miles of public ways and streets in Greenwich.

During the last half century they have increased in small proportion to the growth of the town. The map of Greenwich, from a survey made in October, 1757, and April, 1773, a copy of which appears in Spencer P. Mead's history, shows practically the same highways that are in use to-day.

As a boy and youth I was familiar with all the roads. Many of the old landmarks have disappeared; the dirt road has been changed to macadam; grades have been altered; ancient stone walls have been sacrificed to the greed of the house builder and curves have been eliminated to accommodate the swift moving motor car.

I like to think of them as they were in other days, although we are not without artistic and beautiful highways. But fifty years ago all our roads ran between ancient walls of granite bowlders, softened with the moss of a century and overrun with creeping vines. The stone fences were one of the prettiest features of an afternoon drive. They were as

[306]

crooked in their winding as the track of an adder. They were strangely irregular in shape; some low and some high; some of small stones and some of massive bowlders.

Many of them would have fallen to the ground but for the tenacious grasp of the ivy that ran in and out the fissures of the rock and held them like the strongest mortar.   Some of them were so buried beneath

WOODSEY ROAD

the foliage that only here and there was revealed a glimpse of their mossy surface.   It was hard to believe that they were the creation of man, and not the wild growth of nature.

Many of the roads were shaded and some of them were typical "woodsy roads" where the maiden hair fern would rustle against the spokes of the wheels and the overhanging chestnuts brush against the carriage top.

The farmhouses all had a look of prosperity. The massive chimneys were the style of a century before, when the great open fireplace was the only method of heating the house. Some of the fields were rugged with rocks. The plowman would dodge between the ledges and back and go ahead again with perfect indifference. The soil was sweet and warm between the rocks and the harvest always abundant.

The houses were never connected, by woodsheds,

ROUND HILL WOODSHED

with the barns, as in New Hampshire and in many parts of Massachusetts. The snow has never prevailed sufficiently in these parts to warrant such a construction of farm buildings that a fire in one of them means certain destruction to all.

The woodshed was usually a feature among the farm buildings, although at points near the village it had often been degraded into a storehouse for broken down farm implements, among which the hens would steal their nests and hatch their young, out of season and in open defiance. For what

[308]

farmer's boy would hunt for eggs between the rusty knives of discarded mowing machines? But in the northern part of the town the woodshed continued

to perform its duty of a century earlier. In the fall and early winter it was piled to the roof w i t h seasoning hickory and apple tree wood and its perfume was easily detected. As the shades of evening came on one could see the thin line of wood smoke from the g r e a t chimney and often the odor of flap-jacks came out at the half open door.

ISAAC HOWE MEAD
Snapshot by Nelson B. Mead
1823–1889

The Greenwich farmers always lived well. I used to note the bee skips about the back yard and the milk cans upon pegs in the cleansing sunlight. There were vegetable gardens, apple orchards and melon patches. Rows of Mason jars in the pantry told of how they had everything "in season and out."

[309]

OTHER DAYS IN GREENWICH

In other days the walk to Cos Cob was over the Post Road unless one avoided the dust in summer and the mud in winter by going "across lots" from Davis Landing over the dam and through the Isaac Howe Mead farm, now Bruce Park. In laying out Bruce Park care was taken to preserve all the natural and rustic features of the place, but the removal of the old stone fences and the construction of inviting drives has taken away all the seclusion that its former inaccessibility assured.

CHARLES MEAD
1813–1898

South of the Isaac Howe Mead farm was the farm of Charles Mead, usually known as Mead's Point, for it has a magnificent water front. It had yielded hay and grain to successive generations of Meads. The ancestral home stood not far from the present house owned by his sons, Whitman S. Mead and Charles N. Mead. The old house, which was superseded by the new house longer ago than I can remember, had Dutch doors and a brick oven which told something of the family life of those who lived there more than a century ago. Like all Greenwich farms, it had its potato cellar and once on the keystone of its arch I dug the moss from the words "Noah Mead, 1812." The marks of the chisel revealed the hand of a boy who like the boys of to-day had left his name and the date for future generations to read. The same boy lived to honored manhood and died at the age of seventy-seven.

EDWARD MEAD
1809–1885

Isaac Howe Mead lived in the first brick house built in Greenwich. It stood near the road in front of the present home of William H. Truesdale. Along the lane, for the road was scarcely more, where this house stood, the oaks are very old and thrifty and even in these days artists find many a subject

EDWARD MEAD HOMESTEAD
Built 1832

for their brush. Cos Cob harbor and the Sound are in plain sight and to the northwest one could look across the fields and over the tree tops, now within the enclosure of Milbank, to the village with its tall church spire.

Just north of the Isaac Howe Mead house, on the same road, was a square white house still standing,

JOSEPH BRUSH
1792–1870

but now surrounded by other dwellings which was the home of Lyman Mead. He was prominent in town affairs for many years, and a member of the Legislature.

A little farther along, through a road that retains

all of its former beauty, is the old Post Road at Cos Cob. Opposite the junction of these roads stands one of the old-time mansions, with its four great chimneys and its chaste and artistic front door im-

JOSEPH BRUSH HOMESTEAD BUILT IN THE MIDDLE OF THE EIGHTEENTH CENTURY

This house and the Ephraim Lane, James Waring, and Robert Clark houses were the homes at one time of fifty-three children. In the Brush Homestead were born all of the fourteen children in the family with the exception of Amos, the eldest, who was born in Horseneck

mortalized by Nutting, the artist. It bears the date, 1832. The home of Edward Mead, for many years it was the center of the social life of earlier days when all the children were there to join in the merry times that cannot be forgotten. There is only one Cos Cob in the world, and that is our Cos Cob.

[313]

A few years ago some one—perhaps more than one—conceived the idea of changing the name of Cos Cob to Bayport. An application was made to the Post Office Department, and the name of the office

HOLLY INN, COS COB

was actually changed to the very common name of Bayport. But, fortunately, the railroad company declined to change the name of the station. The school authorities clung to the old name for the district and poor little Bayport was only six feet square, being a small part of a small room, where the residents of Cos Cob went for their daily mail.

There are two very old residences in the center of Cos Cob and once there was an old tide mill. The mill, when it was destroyed by fire January 28, 1899, was one of the oldest buildings in town. The two old

[314]

residences are on opposite sides of the road, the one on the east side being the Joseph Brush homestead which has long since been abandoned as a dwelling. The one on the west, belonging to Mrs. Edward P.

FALLS NEAR THE OLD ROLLING MILL

Holly, is a popular inn. Within its walls are many interesting pieces of antique furniture. The shining brass knocker, on the broad front door, the diminutive window panes, the steep pitch of the rear roof and the massive chimney all tell their story of the long ago.

It is said that artists enjoy this inn and Mr. Hobart B. Jacobs tells me that he knows of no better opportunity for the use of pencil or brush than amid the

[315]

surroundings of Cos Cob. The old mill was a study in itself and many a picture has been drawn of its open door with the grist-laden miller within and the foaming water below, that had "ground the grist and will never turn the wheel again."

An odd kind of a mill is a tide mill, for it will not

ELKANAH MEAD HOMESTEAD

grind except at the ebb of the tide, and to take it at the ebb the miller must ofttimes work at the midnight hour.

Nearby was the Palmer & Duff shipyard. How many years it was the center of activity at Cos Cob! The click of the ship carpenter's hammer and the smell of oakum will never depart from my memory.

Going north from Cos Cob, the Cognewaugh Road always had its attractions. It was narrow and crooked and the hills were steep. The trees hung low and the tangled vines grew close to the track of the wheels. It was along such a road that one would expect to find abandoned farms, but there were

[316]

never any such farms in Greenwich. There were, however, a number of abandoned houses and on more than one occasion I found a spot where a house had sometime stood and nothing remained but a gnarled cherry tree and an overgrown lilac bush, relics of the front dooryard. The locust trees grew on that

road and in the spring the air was heavy with the fragrance of their blossoms.

ELKANAH MEAD
1818–1894

Near some of the abandoned houses were piles of locust, in lengths for posts, looking old and storm-beaten as though they had been entirely forgotten and had no value. Years ago—more than fifty—these small places were occupied by operatives in the rolling mill long ago abandoned.

The Cognewaugh Road enters the North Cos Cob Road, not far from the little settlement, with schoolhouse and church that once went by the name of Dingletown, perhaps because the cow bells were so often heard in that neighborhood. Not far away was the home of Elkanah Mead. It was a great white house visible for half a mile down the road. Here he lived for forty-eight years. He saw his children, that were spared, grow up to honor and cherish him in his declining years. How much of joy and sorrow came to him in this home! So much that it made him the sweet-tempered and genial old man that everyone loved and respected.

The beauty of Greenwich is in its valleys as well as its hills. There is much life and warmth hidden in the meadows and by the brooksides. And in other days most of the farmers appreciated the beauties of nature. It is true they were living in houses, built by earlier generations, who had had no time to look beyond the hay field. In many instances magnificent views had been obstructed by planting apple orchards or by the erection of barns and out-buildings, when perhaps a hundred acres more desirable for such purpose had been left open for culti-vation. But they were always quick to admit the mistake and to point out the prominent knolls on the farm, where a view could be obtained and where, in many instances, have since been built fine residences for city people who appreciate the country.

One of these is Benjamin T. Fairchild, who bought the sightly Caleb W. Merritt home at North Green-wich years before the automobile had made the place accessible and furnished it throughout with Colonial furniture. He may drive or ride one of his fine horses across to Round Hill, but his automobile, never. Down in that deep valley, approached by a tortuous road, runs the infant Byram roaring over the rocks of an ancient millsite. Here in Revo-lutionary days the military operations in Westchester

County and in Western Connecticut were conceived and planned.

The old mill, which long ago disappeared, was the meeting place of the Generals and on one occasion in 1781 Washington himself was present to advise and encourage.

Round Hill was always a fascinating place. It was so quiet, so rural, so peaceful. Perhaps to-day it has as many attractions as in the past, but they are not quite the same. Grand mansions, b e a u t i f u l lawns, tall fences and formidable gateways o c c u p y t h e places of many old houses with well-sweeps in the yards and the simple latch gates that led out to the

CHURCH AT NORTH GREENWICH DESTROYED BY FIRE DEC. 15, 1895

road. In the early morning hours the salty, pungent odor of the sea-marsh, seven miles away, has often been borne to my nostrils by a favorable wind.

Perhaps Saturday night in Round Hill was no different from other weekday nights and yet sometimes as I drove through that quiet hamlet there appeared evidences that the week's work had terminated differently from that of other nights. The farmer boys had tidied up the side-bar buggy and the silver-mounted harness, preparatory to the Sunday drive

[319]

with their best girls. The carriage house doors were still open, while the pool of water by the grassy washstand, the rubber boots and the water-soaked overalls

ODLE C. KNAPP
1815–1888

dripping on their pegs told their own story. Round Hill was a village with a store, a post office and a hill of the same name. To see the hill in all its glory one must ascend it at high noon of a clear October day and look at the horizon of forest, farms and water in one grand sweeping circle. It is now the property of the banker, William Stewart Tod, but once eight acres on the summit belonged to Frederick Bonner, one of the sons of Robert Bonner, of Philadelphia *Ledger* fame.

Fred Bonner was the chum of Alexander Taylor, Jr., and once, when on the latter's steam yacht, *Skylark,* cruising in the Sound he saw through the glasses Round Hill with its single apple tree at the apex. Turning to Taylor he said, "Alex, do you see that land that lies nearer to Heaven than any other in sight? I want to buy it." And within a month it was his.

The old store at Round Hill stood on the west side of the road, in those days, but since it has been moved across the way. It belongs to Nathaniel A. Knapp, but the name "O. C. Knapp" over the door has looked the same since the son was a baby boy, making mud pies with his brothers and sisters in the little pools about the hitching posts.

CHAPTER XXX

RECURRING finally to the farms which constituted rural Greenwich half a century ago, the
Nelson Bush farm, now Belle Haven, comes naturally
to mind. In 1882 this farm was put on the market
at forty thousand dollars. George H. and Henry
Dayton bought six acres of it for $6,000, which
brought the price of the balance down to $34,000.
Subsequently the Belle Haven Land Co. paid that
amount to the Bush heirs and acquired the land. A
tract of twelve acres was also purchased of Augustus
I. Mead for $12,000, located about where the Hackett
Day, Wilbur S. Wright, Thompson and Tyler cottages stand. This made the total original cost of
Belle Haven, before any improvements were made,
about $46,000, quite small compared to the price of
$150,000, paid for the D. Smith Mead farm in 1907.
I visited the ground with about a dozen prospective
stockholders early in the spring of 1883. No finer
day could have been selected for the purpose. There
was just a reminiscence of winter in the air and the
soiled snow lay in ridges along the north side of the
stone walls. But the sun was warm and the twitter
of the bluebirds and the joyful whistle of the meadow
lark, the first of all our song birds, could be heard

across the fields. The matter of the purchase was practically settled that day and Belle Haven, the first residence park that Greenwich ever had, was an as-

NELSON BUSH
1800–1875

sured fact before the cheery trees had blossomed. Before this, land had been divided into building plots such as Rocky Neck, but this was the first land speculation that could really claim the name of a residence park. In 1882 all the land now included in Belle Haven excepting the William H. McCord property

[323]

and about forty acres besides, was assessed for town taxes at $15,490, yielding an annual tax of $193.62. The taxes now paid by the various owners at Belle Haven amount to many thousand dollars. The men who bravely took up the Belle Haven enterprise saw many dark days and in 1885, '86 and '87 the sales were slow and expenses heavy. There were moments, perhaps, when they wished they had taken pronounced views against farm land on that spring day in 1883.

Capt. Thomas Mayo, Nathaniel Witherell and Robert M. Bruce were among the pioneers in the Belle Haven scheme. It is interesting to think of Belle Haven, when it was an open farm many years ago. Once I knew an old man who gave his personal recollections of the place as it appeared early in the last century. On the Byram side of Belle Haven was what was known as the Banks lands, consisting of 29 acres, and after the park was quite well built up, it was bought of Nelson B. Mead for $9,000. This occurred in January, 1889. It was shortly after this that I had an interview with the old man and his recollections are as follows:

"I enjoyed going down there as early as 1820, "when Samuel Bush owned what is now the upper "portion of the park. My recollection of the old "gentleman is very distinct. Never a great talker, "he possessed plenty of ideas and the quaint origi- "nality with which they were expressed, made it worth "all it cost to get them. When alone he said but

[324]

"little, but when I lured him up to Deacon Abraham
"Mead's or down to John Banks' he would talk,
"especially if he got onto the subject of Obadiah
"Banks' will. Obadiah was the father of nine chil-
"dren, all of whom grew to full age, and in the early
"years of the nineteenth century lived in that part of
"Belle Haven purchased of Nelson B. Mead. The old
"man died in 1790. He had been personally inter-
"ested in the Revolutionary war, and the flint-lock
"gun that hung above the mantel had been his pride.
"His son, John Banks, and the widow, Elizabeth,
"never removed it, and I used to see it just as it hung
"when its owner's silent form was carried out of the
"narrow south door for its last resting place. Well,
"Obadiah's will was always an interesting topic for
"Sam Bush and Deacon Abraham Mead. Sam never
"liked it. He used to say that Obadiah's widow
"was altogether too restricted in her rights to the
"farm, and that when he made his will he would pro-
"vide that his widow should have the use of all his
"farm for twenty-one years after his death. And
"that is exactly what he did when he came to make his
"will along in corn-husking time in 1826. But he
"used to complain to the Deacon that the widow Banks
"had too liberal a dower in the use of the house and
"barn which Deacon Mead had set out to her in the
"following language:

" " 'The one-third part of the dwelling house, being
"the west room, with the chamber above said room
"and one-third part of the cellar, with the privi-

"lege of the entry and chamber stairs to go to and
"from said chamber, and to bake in the oven; also
"the one-third part of the barn being the west bay,
"with the liberty of the floor to cart in and through.'

"Sam thought that the mother and girls could
"manage their unity of interest in the oven, but that
"when a sudden shower was coming up and the widow
"and her sons, Ben, Daniel, John and Joshua, were
"each getting in their hay, on their respective parcels,
"they were all likely to get a load to the barn at the
"same time and in the strife for the 'liberty of the
"floor' the hay might get wet. It was certainly a
"small barn for all that was expected of it, and I
"felt a little sorry to hear that it was torn down last
"week. Sam Bush at times would tell us of his boy-
"hood days and how, in the summer evenings, he used
"to sit by Obadiah's west door, and count the potato
"laden sloops sail down the Sound. He thought a
"wonderful sight of Obadiah's children, the oldest of
"whom was quite grown, but the little tow-headed
"ones were a merry lot and they were in and out at
"the door, off to the barn and back, across the knoll
"to the shore, singing and laughing like school chil-
"dren at recess.

"When winter came and the snow fell deep in the
"Field Point Road and drifted across the lane, Dea-
"con Abraham Mead's boys, Isaac and Zophar, ac-
"companied by the Banks boys with their ox team,
"would join forces in breaking the roads. After
"the work was done and the evening chores at the

"barn accomplished, how natural it was for the boys
"to retrace their steps over the newly beaten track
"to Obadiah's home, where the glow of the great open
"fire filled the south room and shone out of the win-
"dows across the snow, to where the tide had tumbled
"the ice against the scarred and seamed rocks along
"the shore.

"The striped cider mug on the shelf, the apple
"basket and the pop corn bag, were not greater at-
"tractions to them than the merry girls gathered in
"a half circle about the hearth.

"I remember well just how the old Banks home-
"stead looked, both without and within. In the cor-
"ner cupboard of the south room was the best blue
"china, that made a beautiful array, and so precious
"that to-day the few pieces that remain would almost
"bring their weight in silver. Their odd but grace-
"ful shapes were decorated with historic scenes, of
"which I recall Washington crossing the Delaware,
"the siege of Yorktown and the landing of Columbus.
"One could eat veal pie and study history at the same
"time.

"Near the china cupboard was a square mahogany
"clock, trimmed with brass, that has long outlived
"its owner, for in a certain office in the village it still
"ticks the time away. Upstairs, the great canopied
"bedsteads were piled high with feathers, and the
"small windows were curtained with the most delicate
"shades of chintz. There were two picture mirrors
"that hung on the wall; one of exquisite design and

"workmanship, representing the fierce marine strug-
"gle between the frigates *Guerriere* and *Constitution*
"in the war of 1812.

"The *Constitution* on even keel, her flags flying,
"but her sails riven with shot, was firing with terrible
"effect upon the hapless *Guerriere* lying almost upon
"her beam ends, with her foremast gone by the
"board, and her severed shrouds hanging over the bul-
"warks.

"Sam Bush bought the mirror in New York in
"1813 for his neighbor, Thomas Hobby, and after Mr.
"Hobby's death John Banks bought it at a vendue.
"The other mirror was much older, but more crude
"in design and workmanship. It represented a girl
"—a grotesque little thing—with a basket on her arm
"and her forefinger in her mouth. Her rosy cheeks
"and red boots were of the same tint and she stood
"out against a yellow background and beneath a
"scarlet canopy.

"For more than twenty-five years after Obadiah
"died, his son, John Banks, occupied the old
"homestead, but his brothers Dan, Joshua, Ben and
"their sister Elizabeth from time to time sold their
"lands to Deacon Abraham Mead, till finally in 1825,
"after the deacon had died, John Banks sold the home-
"stead to Isaac Mead, the son of Abraham Mead and
"the grandfather of Nelson B. Mead."

Just as the old man gave me these facts, with here
and there some verbal changes and the occasional
insertion of a date, I have written them. As I sat

[328]

listening to the story I could see him close his eyes as though visions of the past filled his mind. With the present he showed no sympathy, and expressed no interest except as it pointed to the past and to those who had gone before.

In his anticipations of the future he again saw his

NELSON BUSH HOMESTEAD
Belle Haven

old neighbors. He remembered them as patient, industrious, sober. Their hours of enjoyment, aside from those given to the cultivation of the soil, which was their life, were few. Their integrity was proverbial and their confidence in the honesty and purity of their fellow men, unlimited. Sentiment and affection in their natures were not so much lacking as the ability or disposition to express them.

[329]

A sturdy, honest, reputable race were they of whom their descendants may well be proud and whose sterling qualities very generally have descended to the present generation.

THE END

INDEX

INDEX

Acker, Abraham, 20, 215
Acker, Peter, 20; garden and homestead of, 23, 122, 153
Acker, William, drums up recruits, 130
Adams, Samuel, 5
Aiken, Dr. James, 19, 115
Allen, David K., property of, 289
Allen Brothers, garage of, 267
Allaire Engines, used in marine service, 206, 207
Americus Club, 180, 181, 182, 184, 187, 188, 189, 194; members of, 63, 199, 200, 201, 203, 205, 207, 214
Amogorone, 281
Andrews, Benjamin, 258
Andrews, (Mrs.) Mary E., property of, 94
Andrews, Chief Justice, sitting in trial, Mead will case, opinion of, 50
Anderson, Walter M., property of, 155
Anderson, (Mrs.) A. A., property of, 202
Andrade, Joseph D. C., 200
Apples, become a product of Greenwich farms, 83
Apartment houses, Italian, 32
Arch Street, 26, 117
Ardendale Sanitarium, 226
Artisans, Port Chester, employed in Greenwich, 23
Asten, Peter, 264
Athelcroft, 94
Atwater, Jeremiah W., 282, 284

Bailey, (Mrs.) Henry M., 106
Baker, Edwin H., residence of, 248
Balloon frame building, projection of causes comment, 122
Banks, Benjamin, 326, 328
Banks, Daniel, 326, 328

Banks, (Mrs.) Elizabeth, 325, 328
Banks, John, 44, 325, 326, 328
Banks, (Mrs.) John H., 296
Banks, Joshua, 326, 328
Banks, Obadiah, homestead of, 325, 326, 327; will of, 325, 326
Banks' Homestead, built by Obadiah Peck, 158
Banksville, 61, 117
Banksville stage, connecting link with Greenwich, 61
Baptistry, donated by Wm. M. Tweed, 1869, 223
Barber, Amaziah D., 200
Barker, James, 200
Barnard, George G., 167, 200
Barnum, Henry A., 200
Barnard, John T., 199
Barrow's Point, 213
Bars, unknown in Greenwich, 21
Bassford, Edward D., 199
Bathhouse, The Tweed, 190, 193
Bayport, 314
Beck, Frank S. E., 200
Bedford, 282
Bedford, Gunning S., 200
Bedford stage, stopped at *Stanwich Inn,* 66
Bell, (Mrs.) Alfred, 106
Belle Haven, 322, 323, 324; objection of residents to extension of shore road, 44
Belle Haven Land Co., property of, 322
Belle Haven Park, 205
Benedict, (Miss) Belle, 12
Benedict, Elias C., residence of, 184
Benedict, Henry M., 8, 12, 119, 241, 268; residence of, 155, 158; secures widening of Greenwich Avenue, 120
Benedict Place, 12, 13
Benson, Oliver D., 139
Berrien, Daniel, 200

INDEX

[**334**]

INDEX

Close, Samuel, 18, 35, 37, 93
Coasting, favorite place for, 121
Cognewaugh Road, 316, 317
Cohen, Mayer H., 235; property of, 121, 238
Collier, James W., 200
Colonial Tavern, Mead's, 244
Columbia, District of, compared in size with Greenwich, 25
Company I, Tenth Conn. Volunteers, first to go to war, 130, 133, 137
Committee of Seventy, work of, 161, 174, 176, 229
Congregational Church, old, 19; first edifice, 112: second edifice 1730, 112; third edifice 1798, 112; burning of 1866, 115
Connolly, Richard B., 167, 169, 173, 175
Cooney, William, residence of, 98
Cook, Ada M., property of, 155
Cooper, William, associate of David Mason, 247
Copperheads, Southern sympathizers called, 125
Cornell, Charles G., 199, 264
Corson, Cornelius, 199
Cos Cob, 17, 25, 26, 54, 88, 204, 225, 226, 229, 231, 310, 313, 314, 316; Harbor, 311; River, 300
Coulter, James E., 200
Courtney, (Miss) Hannah, property of, 154, 155, 156
Cozine, John R., 2
Crabs, found at old White Bridge, 60
Crest View, sale of, 94
Cramer Building, 8
Creamer, Thomas J., 201
Cuddy, Edward, 200
Curtis, Julius B., attorney for H. M. Benedict, 19, 120, 134

Daly Building, 274
Dam, the old, 12, 14, 16
Dandy, horse owned by Judge Mead, 34
Danes, population in East Port Chester, 31
Danish Club House, built by Milo Mead, 31
Darrah, John, 213
Davin, Edward A., 199
Davis Avenue, 6, 7, 16, 197, 286

Davis, Abraham B., 2, 5, 259; farm of, 1
Davis' Creek, 54, 300
Davis Cemetery, 57, 60
Davis' Dock, origin of, 68; owned and held by Davis family, 69; litigation over ownership, 69, 70, 71; jury in litigation over ownership, 71; witnesses called in suit over ownership of, 71; ownership of Walter Davis, sustained 1837, 70, 71
Davis, Edward, 304
Davis, Eleanor R., 6; estate of, 6, 69
Davis, Elisha, 303, 304
Davis, Henry, 304
Davis Landing, 2, 217, 310
Davis Lane, 197
Davis Mill, old, 57, 299, 300, 303, 304, 305
Davis, Judge Noah, 176, 177, 227, 228
Davis Pond, 16
Davis, Silas, 2, 258, 259, 304
Davis, Stephen, 303, 304
Davis, Thomas, 303
Davis, Walter, 259, 304
Davidson, John McB., 200
Davison, William, 199
Day, Hackett, residence of, 322
Dayton, George H., property of, 322
Dayton, Henry, property of, 322
Dayton, Jacob, Jr., 70
Dayton, John, 22, 90
Dayton, Mary F., property of, 238
Dearfields, 2, 153
Dearfield, built in 1799, 73; origin of name, 73
Dearfield Drive, origin of name, 73
Deep Hole, 16
Decker, William F., residence of, 85
Delano, (Mrs.) Lucy M., 208
Democratic Party, during war times, 125
Dennis, (Mrs.) Mary, 263
Denson, Frederick, property of, 18
Denton, Humphrey, 252
Derby, Silas, 61, 62; reminiscences of, 62, 63
Dewey, S. Foster, secretary to Wm. M. Tweed, 194, 200
Dewey, William C., 200

INDEX

INDEX

Golden, Ephraim, 70, 71
Gordon, Rev. George A., D.D., pastor of Second Cong. Church, 110, 111
Gould, Jay, 200
Glenville, 244; woolen mills at, 31
Glenville Road, divided Mead farms, 73
Grafulla, Claudius S., 199
Graham, (Miss) Cornelia J., 157
Graham, John, chief counsel for Wm. M. Tweed, 219, 228
Graham, (Miss) Mary E., 157
Grand Jury indicts Wm. M. Tweed, 227
Grant, the Justus Bush, 68, 69
Great Hill, owned by Israel Knapp, 95
Great Island, 256
Greeley, Horace, 264
Green, Andrew H., 175, 176, 229
Green Court Inn, 5
Greenwich Academy, 195, 197, 207, 220
Greenwich Avenue, 7, 20, 22, 23, 118, 123, 137, 219, 222, 233, 242, 245, 249, 266, 267, 274, 286; first purchase of land for business purposes, 22; original widening of, 120
Greenwich Fire Department, 281
Greenwich Hospital, 286; property of, 154
Greenwich Library, 8
Greenwich, Mead's History of, 98
Greenwich & Rye Steamboat Co., formed 1866, 207
Greenwich Savings Bank, 22
Greenwich Trust Co., building of, 23, 122
Grigg, John R., farm of, 32
Grigg Street, 257
Gurney, A., 184
Guion George, 288
Gumbleton, James J., 200

Hagerty, Edwin M., 199
Hall, A. Oakley, 167, 169, 174
Hall, Charles H., 181, 182, 183, 187, 188, 189, 199
Hall, Judge, hands down decision in Davis Dock litigation, 72
Halsey, Schuyler, 200
Hamilton Avenue, 32
Hanan, John H., property of, 32

Hardenbrook, (Miss) Lillie A., property of, 194, 195
Harkness, L. V., property of, 158
Harnett, John H., 200
Harpers' Weekly, 222
Harrison, Joseph G., 200
Harway, James L., 200
Harvey, Alex W., 200
Havemeyer School, 6, 118
Hawley, Charles, attorney Davis' Dock suit, 70, 285
Hawthorne, origin of name, 31
Held House, site of old pottery plant, 38, 257
Held, Henry, meat market of, 23, 122, 123
Hembold, Henry T., 200
Hemlock Woods, 73, 74
Henderson, John, market of, 20
Hendrie, Charles, Jr., property of, 284
Hendrie, J. W., 284
Hermance, Frank, 227
Higgins, A. Foster, 220; property of, 98, 198
Historians, local, XVII
Hitchman, William, 201
Hobby, Captain John, 153, 155
Hobby, Husted, 259
Hobby Tavern, 153, 156
Hobby, Thomas, 328; property of, 155
Hoey, John, 264
Hoey, (Mrs.) John, 264
Hoffman, George W., 229, 230, 231
Hoffman, John T., Mayor of New York 1865, 167, 168
Hogan, Edward, 199
Hoggson, William H., residence of, 253
Holly, Edward P., 106
Holly. (Mrs.) Edward P., 315
Holly, Frank M., M.D., property of, 35, 37
Holly, (Mrs.) Stephen, 106
Holly, William H., 260
Holly Inn, 315
Holmes, Captain Caleb, 26
Holmes, Caleb M., 139
Holmes, (Mrs.) Caleb, 106
Holmes, Frank, 21
Holmes, Reuben, characteristics of, 96; property of, 95
Holmes, Isaac, Jr., 252
Homestead Hall, origin of, 33
Hook lands, the so called, 291

[337]

INDEX

Horse Neck, 26; origin of name, 38
Horse Neck, Hobby property in, 154
Horse Neck Brook, 77; territory near, 37
Horse Neck Field Point, original name, 38
Houses, number built and assessed up to 1859, 25
Howard, Henry Waring, 115
Howe, (Mrs.) Nehemiah, 106
Howe, William A., 106
Hoyt, (Mrs.) Elizabeth R., 106
Hoyt, George H., 268
Hoyt, Col. Heusted W. R., 23, 194, 225
Hoyt, Dr. James H., 267, 268; delivers farewell speech to Co. I, 134
Hubbard, Frederick A., 236; home in 1859, 11
Hubbard, Holly, 137
Hubbard, John, 137
Hubbard, L. P., 241, 268; homestead of, 157
Hubbard, L. P., Jr., enlists in N. H. Regiment, 130
Huelat, Henry H., 199
Hunt, J. Howland, 291
Husted, William A., 259, 262
Hyde, Clarence M., property of, 94
Hyde, Dr. F. C., property of, 90
Hyde, Seymour J., property of, 41

Ice cream, sold in fish market, 23
Ice house, first in town, 34
Indian Chief's Throne, landmark at Rocky Neck, 258
Indian Field, Fresh Air Home at, 84
Indian Harbor, 124, 184, 194, 205; Mead Home at, 38
Indian Harbor Hotel, 184
Indian Harbor Point, 256
Indian Harbor Yacht Club, 26, 261
Ingersoll, James H., 174, 200
Ingersolls', property of, 66
Innis Arden, 280
Inslee, Gage, architect, 188

Jackson, Joseph A., 199

Jackson, Philip N., 230
Jacobs, Hobart B., 315
Jaynes Park, part of Griggs' farm, 33
Jerman, George, 138
Jerman, William, 138
Jerome Park, 218
John Romer, the, 63, 64, 206, 207, 208, 209, 211, 212, 213, 214, 215, 216
Johnson, William, solicits recruits with fife, 130
Jones, Conductor, 277
Jones, Edward, 199
Jones, George, publisher of the *N. Y. Times,* 172, 173, 174
Jones, James E., 200
Jones, Dr. Leander P., 196, 236.
Jones, Morgan, 199
Jones' Stone, 204
June, Theodore, kept boarding school for boys, 67

Kearney, Edward, 199
Keeler, John E., attorney in Mead will case, 47, 48, 49
Keenan, Patrick H., 199
Kernan, Francis, 174
Keyser, John H., 200
Kimmons, John, 187
Kimmons, Richard, 187
King, John T., 199
King, Professor, 264
Kinney, Francis, 199
Kirk, Lewis J., 199
Kirkpatrick, Thomas, 200
Knapp, (Miss) Amelia, 14, 289
Knapp, Brush, 8, 13, 288, 289, 290
Knapp, Caleb, 300
Knapp, Israel, property of, 95
Knapp, (Miss) Martha, 289
Knapp, Nathaniel A., property of, 321
Knapp, Odle C., 233, 321
Koch, Joseph, 200

Laddin's Rock Farm, 285
Lafayette, General, 244
Lafayette Place, 126, 129, 244, 246
Lake Avenue, 207
Lawrence, Charles L., 200
Lawrence, Rt. Rev. William, Bishop of Mass., decries use of stained windows, 65
Leeds, J. W., 267
Lenox House, 20, 156, 244

[**338**]

INDEX

INDEX

Mead, Deacon Abraham, 38, 325, 328

Mead, Alexander, 106

Mead, Alfred, 295

Mead, Allen, 295, 296

Mead, Alvan, 8, 158, 259; property of, 157

Mead, Amos, 245

Mead, Andrew, 92

Mead, (Miss) Anna, 295

Mead, Arthur D., 106

Mead, Augustus, 33

Mead, Augustus, son of Isaac Mead, 38; farm of, 33

Mead, Augustus, son of N. B. Mead, 34; residence of, 226

Mead, Augustus I., 34; property of, 322

Mead, Judge Augustus, 35, 36

Mead, E. Belcher, home of, 91

Mead, Dr. Beverley E., 236, 295

Mead, Caleb, 291, 292

Mead, Caleb, Jr., 291

Mead, (Miss) Catherine, 226

Mead, Charles, 26; farm of, 310

Mead, Charles N., 310

Mead, (Miss) Clarissa, 105

Mead, Cornelius, property of, 288, 291

Mead, (Mrs.) Cornelia J., 90

Mead, Major Daniel Merritt XVII, 22; captain of Co. I, 26, 130; sword presented to, 134; extracts from diary, 133; returns dying, 139; death and funeral of, 140

Mead, (Mrs.) Daniel Merritt, 106

Mead, Daniel S., 120, 259; property of, 117, 190, 257

Mead, Daniel S., Jr., property of, 193

Mead, Daniel Smith, 6

Mead, D. Smith, 6, 246; farm of, 1, 6, 322

Mead, D. Smith, 2nd, 7

Mead, Dr. Darius, 102, 248

Mead, (Mrs.) Deborah, 79

Mead, Drake, 26, 233

Mead, General Ebenezer, sees Gen. Putnam escape from British, 1779, 86

Mead, Rev. Ebenezer, half brother of Theodore H., 87

Mead, Edmund, 295, 296

Mead, Edmund, Jr., 295

Mead, Edward, home of, 226, 227, 229, 230, 313

Mead, (Mrs.) Edward, 105, 106

Mead, Edwin, 7, 286; property of, 120

Mead, Elkanah, administrator, Estate of Judge Mead, 36; homestead of, 317

Mead, (Mrs.) Elsie, 76

Mead, (Miss) Emeline, 295

Mead, (Miss) Eunice, 295

Mead, Frederick, 102; property of, 102, 154, 158, 159, 196, 197

Mead, Hanford, 121

Mead, (Miss) Hannah M., 106

Mead, (Mrs.) Hannah, property of, 96

Mead, (Miss) Hannah R., 80; legacies of, 83

Mead, Henry, 245; property of, 244

Mead, Henry, military funeral of, 139

Mead's History, 306

Mead, Isaac, 38, 326, 328

Mead, Isaac Howe, farm of, 16, 84, 310, 311, 312

Mead, Isaac L., 106, 246; building of, 20

Mead, Irving, 295, 296

Mead, (Mrs.) Jabez, 106

Mead, James, 295

Mead, Jared, property of, 154, 158, 262, 263

Mead, Jeremiah, 291, 292, 295

Mead, Job, 76

Mead, Deacon Jones, 27, 105; death of, 29; Estate of, 27, 29

Mead, Joshua, 96

Mead, (Miss) Laura, 295

Mead, (Mrs.) Laura, 80

Mead, Lot, 26

Mead, (Miss) Louisa, 106

Mead, (Mrs.) Lucy Mumford, 92, 94

Mead, (Miss) Lydia, 295

Mead, Lyman, part donator of sword, 134; homestead of, 312

Mead, Lyman, meadow, 60

Mead, Matthew, 21

Mead, Mark, 27, 29; property of, 32

Mead, Mary Waring, property of, 290

Mead, Merwin, farm of, 14

INDEX

[341]

INDEX

INDEX

Pottery, made by Deacon Abraham Mead, 1790, 43
Prescott Building, 118
Prescourt, owned by H. P. Whittaker, 94
Probate Court, initial judge of, 34; location of, 34, 36, 235
Proprietors, original term applied to taxpayers 1725, 257
Purdy, (Miss) Ann, establishes boarding school, 62
Pumping station, the new, 54
Putnam Avenue, 2, 17, 18, 20, 35, 115, 120, 153, 198, 222, 233, 234, 244, 267, 286, 288
Putnam Cottage, 95, 98
Putnam, General, 90, 244
Putnam Hill, 86, 87, 153, 155, 218, 248
Putnam Terrace, 14
Pyne, John, 200

Radford, Stephen L., 26
Radicals, Republicans called, 125
Railroads, early, 266, 267, 268, 269, 270, 273, 274, 275, 276, 277, 278, 279
Railway stations, four in Greenwich, 25
Randall's Island, orphan children from, visit *Linwood,* 222
Ray, George S., wheelwright, 93
Read, Charles B., 74
Read, Ephraim, 180; property of, 261
Red Rock, 209
Regattas, in Tweed's day, 203
Reynolds, Abraham, 26
Reynolds, Augustus N., 26
Reynolds, (Mrs.) Augustus N., 106
Reynolds, Gideon, 106
Reynolds, Frank, V. R., house of, 13, 14
Reynolds, (Mrs.) William T., 106
Riker's Island, 213
Ritch, Thomas, 150; property of, 219
Ritch, (Mrs.) Thomas, 106
Rivers, (Miss) Frances M., 151
Riverside, 25, 280, 282
Roads, ancient, 306, 307, 308, 310
Rogers, William C., 200
Round Hill, 37, 117
Round Hill Farms Dairy, 129
Robbins, George, 138
Robbins, William, 138

Roche, Walter, 199
Rockefeller Park, 8, 220
Rockefeller, Percy A., property of, 253
Rockefeller, William G., property of, 253
Rock Ridge, 73, 76; oldest house in, 78; appraised value of, 83; sale of, 84; becomes site of Fresh Air Home for children, 85
Rocky Neck, 26, 117, 183, 190, 257, 258, 323
Rocky Neck Company, the, 257, 259, 260, 262, 265
Rocky Neck Point 1836, Map of, 256
Rocky Point, 184
Rockwood Lake, 65
Root, Elihu, junior counsel for Wm. M. Tweed, 219
Rosevelt, George W., 199
Roslyn, 213
Round Island, 111, 180, 182, 183, 256; potato cellar on, 83, 182, 262; owned by Oliver Mead, 41; proposed purchase by Town of, 44
Round Hill, 288, 318, 319, 320, 321
Runyan, (Mrs.) Fanny, 263, 264
Rural free delivery, before days of, 25
Russell, Joseph E., 93
Russell, (Mrs.) Joseph E., 106
Ryan, James, 200
Rye Beach, 63

Sackett, (Mrs.) Anna, 253
Sackett, Henry, farm of, 274
Sackett, Justus, 252
Sackett, Justus, Jr., 253
Sackett, Justus Ralpn, 254
Sackett, William H., 253
Sand's Point, 263
Sanitary Commission, has branch in Greenwich, 138
Sarah Thorp, the, 215
Satterlee, John, 200
Sawpits, 256
Sayles, Solomon, 200
Schaffer, Christian W., 199
Schaffer, John, 138
Schaffer, Louis, 138
Schaffer, William H., 199
Schifferdecker, Henry, 305

[343]

INDEX

INDEX

[345]

INDEX